Pizza
on a
Plank

Pizza
on a
Plank

Make Wood-Fired
Pizza on Your Grill!

Dina Guillen

Workman
Workman Publishing
Hachette Book Group, Inc.
1290 Avenue of the Americas
New York, NY 10104
workman.com

Workman is an imprint of Workman Publishing, a division of Hachette Book Group, Inc.
The Workman name and logo are registered trademarks of Hachette Book Group, Inc.

Design by Rae Ann Spitzenberger
Cover photo by Randazzo & Blau

The publisher is not responsible for websites (or their content) that are not owned by the publisher.

Workman books may be purchased in bulk for business, educational, or promotional use.
For information, please contact your local bookseller or the Hachette Book Group
Special Markets Department at special.markets@hbgusa.com.

Library of Congress Cataloging-in-Publication Data is available.
ISBN 978-1-5235-2498-3

First Edition April 2025

Printed in China on responsibly sourced paper.

10 9 8 7 6 5 4 3 2 1

A NOTE ON SAFETY
Plank grilling produces smoke and is not intended for indoor grilling. If you
have questions or require more information about a plank grilling product,
please contact the manufacturer directly. Planks used for grilling may
catch fire, so please always have a spray bottle filled with water readily
available when plank grilling to put out any fires. Neither the author nor
the publisher will be liable for any consequences, losses, or damages
arising out of any use or application of the recipes contained in this book.

For Roland
and Andrew

Contents

Preface

Gourmet thin crust wood-fired pizza. Until now, this was a dish you'd find only on a restaurant menu unless you installed a costly outdoor wood-burning pizza oven in your backyard. But what if you could convert your barbecue into a wood-fired pizza oven with just one slab of wood? Good news: With an inexpensive grilling plank, you can! The wooden plank transforms your pizza into something so delicious, it will be the only way you will want to prepare a homemade pizza from now on. Trust me, this is a game changer. The crust comes out crispy, chewy, and lightly blistered. Plus, both toppings and crust achieve a whole new level of flavor perfection after being kissed by smoke.

I had no idea what I was getting into when I started plank grilling. About twenty years ago, my brother Sam called me with an urgent request. He owned a grilling plank manufacturing company, and many of his customers were writing to him, asking how to use the slabs of wood they had just purchased from Williams Sonoma or Sur La Table. (Plank grilling has become a lot more popular since then, and planks can now be readily purchased at many other major retailers, like Walmart, Costco, The Home Depot, Amazon, and even your local grocery store.) Sam knew I was a writer and that I loved cooking, so he asked if I would write a few recipes to package with his planks and send to his customers. What started as "a few" recipes has turned into my third cookbook on plank grilling.

I've grilled practically everything on a plank. From meatloaf to corn on the cob to pork chops, plank grilling unlocks the full flavor potential of every dish. But it is pizza that my friends and family keep requesting again and again. I started with simple yet delicious cheese pizzas, but then I found myself converting leftover brisket into a barbecued brisket planked pizza and leftover chicken into an Indian-inspired butter chicken planked pizza. The smoke emanating from the grilling plank, and the wood itself, infuse the dough, cheese, and sauce on every pizza, ensuring that every bite is a flavor bomb.

> **Plank grilling is fun, and anything that makes it stressful should be taken out of the process.**

My favorite recipes are those that I customize to my own tastes, so consider this cookbook a starting place. If you see a recipe that calls for pork and you prefer chicken, go ahead and make the substitution. In fact, I've included notes on many of the recipes that offer suggestions about how to make them your own. And if you don't feel like making your own dough or sauce from scratch, "store-bought is fine," as Ina Garten, one of my favorite cookbook authors, says. Plank grilling is fun, and anything that makes it stressful should be taken out of the process. Say goodbye to boring homemade pizza and hello to your new go-to method.

Happy plank grilling!

Getting Started

Are you ready to impress your dinner guests with the flavor and aroma of a planked pizza? Grilling pizza on a wood plank may sound intimidating, but with the right know-how, you can do it like a pro. You may be wondering whether your grill is even fit for plank grilling. The answer is "yes"—whether you have a gas or charcoal grill, you can achieve the tastiest planked pizzas. Gas grills are my personal preference because I find controlling the heat and flame easier, but if you have a charcoal grill, simply create an indirect heat setup, keeping one side hot and the other cool. Get your hands on some food-safe grilling planks, and you're on your way.

TYPES OF PLANKS

When it comes to choosing planks for grilling pizzas, some of my favorites are maple, alder, and cherry, and all the recipes in this book were prepared on all three woods. They have slightly sweeter flavor profiles and pair well with pizzas. Cedar planks are the most commonly found in stores, but I find cedar too sweet, and prefer to save my cedar planks to grill fish and vegetables. If you're not sure what types of woods you would prefer with pizza, invest in a variety pack and do some experimenting.

SOAKING THE PLANK

This is perhaps the most critical step. An unsoaked plank can incinerate in high heat—burning your food along with it. Start by using a clean, untreated piece of wood. Most of the planks sold in stores vary in thickness, from a little under ½ inch thick to 1 inch thick. Lengthwise, make sure the plank is large enough to fit the size of your pizza, but small enough that you can close the lid of your grill. All the pizzas in this book were prepared on a plank that was 13 inches long by 7 inches wide and about ⅜ inch thick.

No matter the size, plan on soaking your plank for at least one hour and up to twenty-four hours. The added moisture makes the plank resist burning, which prolongs its use. For the soaking vessel, use a kitchen sink, a cooler, a generously sized glass or ceramic baking dish, or any container large enough to fit your grilling plank. Weigh down the wood with something heavy, like a brick, so it stays submerged during the soaking process.

PREHEATING THE PLANK

Once you've soaked your plank, it's necessary to preheat it. With woods like maple, oak, cherry, and alder, the plank will often begin to warp when placed over heat (cedar does not usually warp). Preheating the plank controls the warping, kills any bacteria on the cooking surface, and imparts a more intense flavor to the food.

For a gas grill, preheat your grill to medium-high, about 475°F.

For a charcoal grill, fill a smokestack/chimney starter to the top with charcoal. Light it and let it burn until half of the coals are glowing. Prepare for indirect grilling by spreading the coals onto half of the bottom of the grill, leaving the other side empty. Place the lid on your grill and fully open the top and bottom vents. If the grill does not have a thermometer, place a grill thermometer through one of the vent openings and let it sit for five minutes to get an accurate reading. You want the temperature at 475°F. If

the grill gets too hot, partially close the vents and let the temperature adjust. Continue adjusting the vent opening until 475°F is maintained consistently.

Before placing the plank on the grill, have a spray bottle with water handy to smolder any flare-ups. Place the plank on the grill and begin preheating the wood. Once you see some light wisps of gray smoke emanating from the grill after one or two minutes, open the grill lid and flip the plank over. If the plank has not bowed, you are ready to begin grilling. If warping occurs, flip the plank, close the lid again, and continue preheating another minute or two until the plank flattens out. Repeat this step once or twice as needed until the warping is controlled.

I SEE BLACK SMOKE!

Always have water nearby—a spray bottle, a hose, anything that can smother flames—in case the plank catches on fire. If it does catch, carefully open the lid and examine the size of the fire. Small fires can be put out quickly by dousing them with water. For a larger fire, remove the pizza from the plank using a pizza peel or spatula, move it to a nearby baking sheet, then remove the plank from the grill using grilling tongs and extinguish the fire as quickly as possible. If the plank is intact, replace it on the grill, move the pizza back on to the plank, close the lid, and continue grilling.

PREP THE PLANKS

1 Weight the planks with a heavy object while soaking.

2 Preheat the soaked plank on both sides with the grill lid closed.

3 A bowed plank needs to be flattened before it's used.

4 Flip the plank with tongs, close the lid, and preheat until it flattens.

ARRANGE THE DOUGH

1 Sprinkle the plank with cornmeal, then unroll the dough.

2 Stretch the dough to fit the plank, making sure it doesn't hang over.

3 Prick the dough with a fork before grilling.

4 Add the toppings after the dough has grilled for 5 to 7 minutes.

MONITORING THE SMOKE

When it comes to plank grilling, smoke is your friend but not just any old friend; it's your best friend. Without smoke, you don't get the full benefits of plank grilling. So once the pizza is placed on the wood and the grill lid is closed, monitoring the smoke is key. You want to see a consistent, steady stream of light-gray smoke coming off the plank or through the grill vent. Billowing black smoke is a sign that the plank may be on fire.

GRILLING PIZZA ON THE PLANK

Start grilling by placing the dough on the toasted side of the preheated plank. I like to grill the dough for several minutes before adding the toppings. Don't flip the dough while grilling on the plank. It's like trying to flip a loaf of bread while it's baking in your oven—there's no need. Always close the grill lid and vigilantly monitor the smoke. If the smoke dissipates when you place food on the plank, raise the heat or open the grill vents until you begin to see light-gray to white smoke emanating from the grill. Once the smoke is a light gray, lower the heat.

Keep monitoring the smoke throughout the grilling process to maintain that light-gray color. The grilling time in each recipe is based on the light-gray smoke indicating a consistent temperature between 475° to 500°F. But each grill is different, so don't rely on the thermometer as much as your eyes.

Keep the grill lid closed throughout the grilling process. Closing the lid allows the food to cook evenly and retain moisture. Think of your grill like an oven—every time you open it, heat escapes. With plank grilling, you have the added consequence of a fire starting from the air entering the heated space. It is the most difficult part of plank grilling, but don't be tempted to peek. Let the natural humidity of the wood envelop the pizza, let the smoke do its magic, and the results will be worth it!

REUSING THE PLANK

Grilling planks can be used multiple times—I have made four to five pizzas with a single piece of wood. As long as the plank is intact, it can be used again and again until it is completely charred and crumbling. If using the plank multiple times in the same day, there is no need to soak it between pizzas. After removing the first cooked pizza from the plank, simply roll out more dough on the plank and make the next one.

To store used planks, wash them well with hot water (do not use soap), place them in a large plastic bag while still wet, and store them in the freezer. When grilling on a used plank, soak and preheat it just like you would a new one.

Once a used plank is completely charred, you can crumble it and spread the pieces on the bottom of the grill to use as smoking chips.

14 Tips for the Best Planked Pizzas

1. Avoid windy days when plank grilling. Wind will kick up the flames and often result in a plank fire when you lift the grill lid to add dough or toppings.

2. Try to use a scale when measuring the dough ingredients, especially when measuring flour, since flour is compacted in the bag. If a kitchen scale isn't available, spoon the flour into a measuring cup and level off the top with the back of a knife.

3. Don't use cold dough. Remove your dough from the refrigerator two to four hours before grilling so it has time to come to room temperature. If the dough is coming from the freezer, thaw it in the refrigerator one day ahead, then let it sit at room temperature for two to four hours before grilling.

4. No rolling pin needed. Instead of rolling out your dough with a rolling pin, use your hands to gently pull and stretch the dough into a rectangle the size of your plank. Rolling the dough deflates the air bubbles and creates a tougher crust. If the dough is resistant to stretching or begins to tear, set it on the counter for ten minutes covered with plastic wrap, then resume stretching. And don't worry if it's not a perfect rectangle—just make sure that when placing the dough on the plank, it doesn't hang over the edges.

5. Stretch it thin. You want your dough to be thin in the center and thicker on the outer edges. If your dough is too thick, it will burn on the outside before it cooks all the way through.

6. Have a spray bottle filled with water nearby while plank grilling. Flare-ups can (and do) occur.

7. Go hot or go home. Grill your pizzas at 475° to 500°F. Any cooler, you might not get the amount of smoke needed to infuse the pizzas. Any hotter, and the wood plank may catch on fire. That being said, monitor your grill closely, as grills vary widely. Rely more on the level of smoke emanating from your grill than a thermometer reading—a watchful eye is better than a grill thermometer. You want to see a constant, steady stream of light-gray smoke while grilling the pizza.

8. Fold and carry. Instead of using a pizza peel to transport the dough to the grill, I find it easier to fold the dough and hand carry it. I sprinkle the plank with cornmeal and unroll the dough onto the plank. Wearing heat-resistant gloves to protect your hands and forearms is a good idea, too.

9. Grill first, top second. Unless otherwise noted, always grill and crisp the dough before adding the toppings, otherwise the crust will be too soft and soggy when it comes off the grill.

———

10. Be prepared. Assemble and/or cook your toppings ahead of time and place them beside the grill before you put the dough on the plank. Precooking ingredients concentrates their flavors and helps cook out some of their moisture. Chop, mix, and measure all the ingredients that are going on the pizza, organize them in dishes, and place them on a nearby tray. After your initial grill of the dough, quickly assemble the ingredients on the crust, close the grill lid, and continue grilling the pizza until the cheese is melted and bubbly and the ingredients are warmed through.

———

11. Tread lightly. While there are measurements for every ingredient in the pizza recipes, less is more when it comes to sauces and toppings. You don't want the pizza weighed down by its ingredients, so use them sparingly. All the pizzas in this book are prepared on a 13-by-7-inch wood plank using 9 ounces of dough. If your plank is smaller, use less dough, sauce, and toppings than the recipe suggests.

———

12. Assemble your tools. If you are using the plank as your serving platter after grilling, have a baking sheet ready by the grill so you can transfer the plank and pizza once it's done cooking. Use tongs or oven mitts to move the planked pizza to the baking sheet. Once the pizza cools for ten minutes, it can be sliced directly on the plank.

13. It's OK to reuse a plank. If you're preparing more than one pizza at a time, you can use the same plank without resoaking it while the grill is still hot. Remove the first pizza from the plank (I use a pizza peel and tongs), then sprinkle cornmeal and place the dough for the next pizza on the same plank. If the plank looks warped, just flip it over, place the dough on the charred side, and continue with the recipe.

———

14. Feel free to tinker. Pizza is one of the easiest meals to adjust for dietary restrictions because store-bought gluten-free and low-carb crusts are readily available. If the crust is already cooked, as many commercial cauliflower crusts are, simply skip the initial dough grilling in the recipe. Preheat the grill as stated, place the precooked dough on the plank, top it, and plank grill it as directed.

———

Doughs & Sauces

There are people who say it's the dough that makes a good pizza. Others say it's the sauce or the quality of the cheese and other ingredients. I'm in camp dough. I'm also in camp thin crust. I've included three different doughs in this book, and they're all thin crust doughs because that's what tastes the best when plank grilled—they get really crispy and chewy, which is what I love when biting into a thin crust pizza.

They are also all no-knead doughs that are mixed in a food processor. If I read a dough recipe that says "knead with your hands," I turn the page. I prefer the food processor over a stand mixer because it kneads the dough quickly (in less than a minute), and it warms the dough, which makes it rise faster. You can use these doughs the day they are made, but I recommend letting them sit at least overnight, and up to three days, in the refrigerator before you use them. The flavor and texture of the dough comes out so much better when it is allowed to ferment for longer.

Each dough recipe makes enough for about three pizzas. If you don't plan on using all three balls of dough, wrap the remaining balls individually in 1-quart resealable bags and freeze for up to three months. Just take the dough out of the freezer the day before to defrost in the fridge, and let it come to room temperature for two to four hours before you grill your pizzas.

My passion for dough notwithstanding, I have a sauce habit. Pizzas aren't ready to be consumed until there's a sauce that brings the entire pie together, even if it's just a drizzle of hot honey or balsamic glaze. The sauces in this book were created to complement the flavors of wood and smoke. These sauces carefully balance sweet and savory to elevate all the toppings and pair perfectly with plank-grilled pizzas.

Tomato sauce is a pizza staple, and I've included a Crushed Tomato Sauce (page 29) that can be used as a base for Italian, Mexican, Middle Eastern, Korean, and other delicious pizza versions found in this book. If you normally veer toward red-sauced pizzas, the Garlic Cream Sauce (page 30) and Pesto Sauce (page 33) will inspire you to embrace variety. These outliers often don't get the credit they deserve since red sauce pizzas get all the attention, but I love that they beautifully showcase all kinds of toppings and make some of the best tasting pizzas.

My ideal pizzas are ones finished with a light drizzle, that perfect touch that brings it all together. The Hot Honey and Balsamic Glaze recipes (page 34 and 35, respectively) can be used for almost any pizza in this book, so keep a stash in your refrigerator for easy access.

PREP DOUGH FOR GRILLING

When the dough is ready, shape it on a well-floured work surface. Begin stretching it with your hands into a rectangle or oval slightly larger than the plank—avoid a rolling pin, which will make the crust tough. As you stretch the dough, move it around to ensure it will slide off the surface easily. If the dough is springing back on you, let it rest for a few minutes, then return to it and stretch as thinly as possible. I find the best way to transport dough to the grill is by folding it in thirds, making it easier to lift and carry. Here's how to do it:

① Gently begin pulling and stretching the dough with your hands.

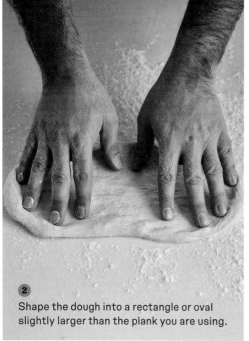

② Shape the dough into a rectangle or oval slightly larger than the plank you are using.

③ As you stretch the dough, move it around to prevent sticking.

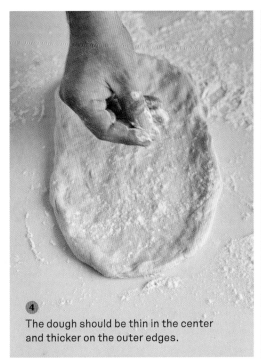

4 The dough should be thin in the center and thicker on the outer edges.

5 Fold one side of the dough into the center.

6 Fold the other side toward the center, overlapping the previous fold as you would a letter.

7 The pizza dough is ready to be transported to the preheated plank.

Neapolitan-Style Dough

Choose this dough when only a few ingredients are going on your pizza—such as Four Cheese Pizza (page 39) and Pizza Margherita (page 40)—and a sturdy crust is not needed. When shaping this dough, the center should be flat and thin and the edges should be thicker to achieve a chewy, charred crust while grilling. Try using Italian-style "00" flour, which makes it easier to stretch the dough thin. You can find it at some supermarkets as well as online at Kingarthurbaking.com and Amazon.

1 Combine the yeast and warm water in a medium bowl and whisk for 30 seconds, or until the yeast dissolves. Set aside for 5 to 10 minutes to give the yeast time to bloom.

2 Place the flour and salt in the bowl of a food processor and pulse five or six times until combined. With the food processor on, slowly pour in the yeast mixture. Process until a ball forms, about 15 seconds. Continue to process for another 15 seconds.

3 Lightly grease a large bowl with the oil. Transfer the dough to the prepared bowl, cover with plastic wrap, and let rise at room temperature until doubled in size, 1 to 2 hours.

4 Punch down the dough, cut it into thirds, and grill as directed in each recipe (see Note).

Makes 27 ounces (765 g), enough for three 9-ounce (250 g) balls of dough (about 3 pizzas if using a 13-by-7-inch plank)

1½ teaspoons active dry yeast (see box, page 23)

1¼ cups (300 ml) plus 3 tablespoons warm water (100° to 110°F)

3¾ cups (500 g) Italian-style "00" flour or all-purpose flour

1½ teaspoons kosher salt (see box, page 25)

Neutral oil , such as vegetable,canola, corn, avocado

Note: *If preparing the dough ahead of time, spray the inside of three 1-quart resealable plastic bags with cooking spray, then place one ball of dough in each prepared bag. Seal and refrigerate for 24 to 72 hours. Remove the dough from refrigerator and let it stand at room temperature for 2 to 4 hours before making the pizza. If not using the dough within 72 hours, it can be frozen, tightly sealed in bags, for up to 3 months. Defrost the dough overnight in the refrigerator, then bring it to room temperature 2 to 4 hours before making the pizza.*

THE WORD ON YEAST

There are three popular types of baker's yeast used in pizza-making: active dry, instant, and fresh. All of them work great to leaven dough, so it all comes down to personal preference when choosing which one to use. Active dry and instant yeasts have a much longer shelf life and can be stored at room temperature, while fresh yeast must be refrigerated and used within a week or two. Fresh and instant yeast do not need blooming or proofing time and can be added directly into the dough, but active dry yeast requires blooming before being incorporated into the dough. To bloom the active dry yeast, simply whisk it into warm liquid—it will begin to foam. If it hasn't formed a light foam after 10 minutes, it needs to be thrown away.

I prefer to use active dry yeast because I can tell whether the yeast has leavening power before taking the time to make the dough and running the risk of it not rising. I also prefer active dry yeast for slower-rising, no-knead doughs. I recommend proofing your dough at least overnight in the refrigerator.

New York–Style Dough

This thin crust dough is supple and tender and crisps up nicely because of the addition of oil and honey. It's also a sturdy crust, so if you're making a pizza with a lot of toppings (like the Crispy Brussels Sprouts and Roasted Tomato Pizza with Garlic Cream Sauce and Balsamic Glaze, page 79, or the Eggplant Caponata Pizza, page 112), this is the dough to choose.

Makes 27 ounces (765 g), enough for three 9-ounce (250 g) balls of dough (about 3 pizzas if using a 13-by-7-inch plank)

2 tablespoons extra virgin olive oil, plus more for greasing the bowl

1 tablespoon honey

1½ teaspoons active dry yeast (see box, page 23)

1¼ cups (300 ml) warm water (100° to 110°F)

3¾ cups (500 g) all-purpose flour

1½ teaspoons kosher salt (see box, page 25)

1 Combine the 2 tablespoons of oil, honey, yeast, and warm water in a medium bowl and whisk for 30 seconds. Set aside for 5 to 10 minutes to give the yeast time to bloom.

2 Place the flour and salt in the bowl of a food processor and pulse five or six times until combined. With the food processor on, slowly pour in the yeast mixture. Process until the mixture forms a ball, about 15 seconds. Continue to process for another 15 seconds.

3 Lightly grease a large bowl with oil. Transfer the dough to the prepared bowl, cover with plastic wrap, and let rise at room temperature until doubled in size, 1 to 2 hours.

4 Punch down the dough, cut it into thirds, and grill as directed in each recipe.

Note: *If preparing the dough ahead of time, spray the inside of three 1-quart resealable plastic bags with cooking spray, then place one ball of dough in each prepared bag. Seal and refrigerate for 24 to 72 hours. Remove the dough from refrigerator and let it stand at room temperature for 2 to 4 hours before making the pizza. If not using the dough within 72 hours, it can be frozen, tightly sealed in bags, for up to 3 months. Defrost the dough overnight in the refrigerator, then bring it to room temperature 2 to 4 hours before making the pizza.*

SALT MATTERS

There are two major brands of kosher salt found in grocery stores: Diamond Crystal and Morton's Kosher salt. There is a big difference in grain size and saltiness between the two, and it's important to adjust the amounts if swapping out one for the other. The recipes in this book were developed using Diamond Crystal, which has smaller crystals and is crumblier, whereas Morton's is denser and saltier. If you have Morton's Kosher or another brand in your spice cabinet, you may want to adjust the measurement. Note that 1 teaspoon Morton's Kosher salt has the same saltiness as 1¾ teaspoons Diamond Crystal salt.

Beer Pizza Dough

Pizza dough made with beer yields a dough that is chewier and fluffier as a result of the carbonation. Lagers and pale ales make a dough with a lighter, earthy flavor (I'd pair the Buffalo Chicken Pizza, page 67, with this dough) while IPAs and stouts give the dough a more pronounced beer flavor (the Meatball and Tomato Pomegranate Pizza, page 51, works great with this kind of dough)—even hard ciders work well. Just choose a beer that you would drink on its own.

Makes 27 ounces (765 g), enough for three 9-ounce (250 g) balls of dough (about 3 pizzas if using a 13-by-7 inch plank)

2 tablespoons extra virgin olive oil, plus more for greasing the bowl

1 tablespoon honey

1½ teaspoons active dry yeast (see box, page 23)

1¼ cups (300 ml) warm beer (100° to 110°F)

3¾ cups (500 grams) all-purpose flour

1½ teaspoons kosher salt (see box, page 25)

1 Combine the 2 tablespoons of oil, the honey, yeast, and beer in a medium bowl and whisk for 30 seconds. Set aside for 5 to 10 minutes to give the yeast time to bloom.

2 Place the flour and salt in the bowl of a food processor and pulse five or six times until combined. With the food processor on, slowly pour in the yeast mixture. Process until the mixture forms a ball, about 15 seconds. Continue to process for another 15 seconds.

3 Lightly grease a large bowl with oil. Transfer the dough to the prepared bowl, cover with plastic wrap, and let rise at room temperature until doubled in size, 1 to 2 hours.

4 Punch down the dough, cut it into thirds, and grill as directed in each recipe.

Note: *If preparing the dough ahead of time, spray the inside of three 1-quart resealable plastic bags with cooking spray, then place one ball of dough in each prepared bag. Seal and refrigerate for 24 to 72 hours. Remove the dough from refrigerator and let it stand at room temperature for 2 to 4 hours before making the pizza. If not using the dough within 72 hours, it can be frozen, tightly sealed in bags, for up to 3 months. Defrost the dough overnight in the refrigerator, then bring it to room temperature 2 to 4 hours before making the pizza.*

Crushed Tomato Sauce

This sauce is the base for most of the red sauce pizzas in this book. Keep a batch in your refrigerator, and you're set to make a last-minute pizza any time. This recipe can easily be doubled or tripled when feeding a large group. **Makes 1 cup**

1½ tablespoons extra virgin olive oil

2 garlic cloves, minced

1 cup canned crushed tomatoes

¼ teaspoon kosher salt (see box, page 25)

¼ teaspoon freshly ground black pepper

1   Heat the oil in a medium skillet or saucepan over medium heat. Add the garlic and cook, stirring often, for 30 seconds. Stir in the tomatoes, salt, and pepper and cook until the tomato mixture slightly thickens and becomes saucy, about 10 minutes.

2   Use the sauce as directed in the pizza recipe of your choice. If not using right away, let it sit until it reaches room temperature, then store it in a glass jar in the refrigerator. It will keep for up to 1 week. It also freezes well. Pour the room temperature sauce into a freezer-safe bag, removing as much air as possible, and store it flat in the freezer for up to 6 months.

Garlic Cream Sauce

I adore white sauce pizzas and their creamy ooziness. This sauce is spiked with garlic and black pepper for extra flavor and is the base for all the white sauce pizzas in this book. The recipe can be doubled or tripled for multiple pizzas. **Makes 1 cup**

1 cup heavy cream

2 garlic cloves, smashed and peeled

¼ teaspoon kosher salt (see box, page 25)

¼ teaspoon freshly ground black pepper

2 teaspoons unsalted butter, at room temperature

2 teaspoons all-purpose flour

1 Combine cream, garlic, salt, and pepper in a small saucepan and bring to a boil over medium-high heat. Reduce the heat to low and simmer for 10 to 12 minutes, or until slightly thickened. In the meantime, mix the butter and flour with a fork in a small bowl until they're combined and look like a paste, then whisk the butter mixture into the warmed cream. Cook until thickened, about 30 seconds. Remove the garlic with a spoon and discard.

2 Use the sauce as directed in the pizza recipe of your choice. If not using right away, this sauce will keep in the refrigerator for up to 5 days in a plastic container or glass jar. It will thicken as it cools, so when ready to use, rewarm it in a microwave for 20 to 30 seconds, until spreadable. It is best not to freeze cream sauces since separation can occur.

Pesto Sauce

Plank-grilled pizza with pesto sauce is the ultimate summer meal. I've added a little bit of lemon juice to this recipe, which gives the sauce just a hint of brightness to complement the smoke in the pizzas. **Makes 1 cup**

1   Place the pine nuts and garlic in the bowl of a food processor and pulse several times. Add the basil, Parmesan, salt, and pepper. Pulse several more times, scrapping down the sides of the food processor with a rubber spatula. With the processor running, slowly pour the oil and lemon juice through the feed tube in a slow stream and process until emulsified and smooth. Avoid pouring the oil too quickly because it will result in a separated sauce.

2   Use as directed in the pizza recipe of your choice. If not using right away, this sauce will keep in the refrigerator for up to 7 days in a plastic container or glass jar. This sauce also freezes well—just make sure it is sealed tightly in a freezer bag so air doesn't oxidize the basil and turn it brown.

⅓ cup pine nuts, toasted (see box)

3 garlic cloves, coarsely chopped

2 cups packed fresh basil leaves

½ cup (1 ounce) freshly grated Parmesan

½ teaspoon kosher salt (see box, page 25)

¼ teaspoon freshly ground black pepper

½ cup extra virgin olive oil

1 tablespoon fresh lemon juice

HOW TO TOAST NUTS

To toast the pine nuts, or any nut, add them to a dry skillet (no oil) over medium heat. Cook them, stirring often, until they're golden brown and smell nutty, about 3 minutes. Whatever you do, don't walk away from the stove because nuts burn easily. Once toasted, transfer the nuts to a plate or bowl so they don't continue cooking.

MAKE IT YOUR OWN

Substitute other toasted nuts like walnuts, pistachios, pecans, or cashews for the toasted pine nuts, or try making this pesto with sunflower seeds instead of nuts. You can also use roasted garlic instead of fresh garlic. If you're low on basil, add parsley or spinach to make up volume; spinach and parsley keep the pesto greener for longer—basil tends to darken quickly.

Hot Honey

This spicy, sweet honey goes so well with smoky plank-grilled pizzas. If you feel adventurous and want to play with the flavors of the honey, try substituting chopped chipotle, gochujang, or sriracha to taste for the red pepper flakes. **Makes 1 cup**

1 cup honey

2 teaspoons red pepper flakes

1 teaspoon apple cider vinegar

1 Combine the honey and red pepper flakes in a small saucepan over medium-low heat and stir to evenly distribute the pepper flakes. Cook for 5 to 10 minutes to infuse the flavors. Remove the pan from the heat and stir in the vinegar. Allow the honey to sit for a few minutes, then taste. If you want it spicier, let it sit longer. The longer you let the red pepper flakes infuse the honey, the spicier it will be. Once it's to your liking, strain the honey to remove the red pepper flakes.

2 Once cooled, transfer the hot honey to a jar or container. Store at room temperature for up to a month.

Balsamic Glaze

A drizzle of balsamic glaze adds a touch of sweetness and nonaggressive acidity that pairs wonderfully with strawberries and tomatoes. You will only need one to two tablespoons of the glaze to elevate a pizza from *great* to *wow*, so store the remaining glaze for up to a month in the refrigerator. **Makes ½ cup**

1 cup balsamic vinegar

2 tablespoons honey or light brown sugar (optional)

1   Pour the vinegar into a small saucepan and heat over medium heat. Stir in the honey, if desired, for a sweeter glaze. Bring the mixture to a gentle boil, then reduce the heat to low and simmer, uncovered, for 15 to 20 minutes, until the glaze thickens and is reduced by half. Stir occasionally to prevent burning and ensure even reduction.

2   Remove the pan from the heat and let cool for a few minutes. As the glaze cools, it will thicken even more. Once the glaze has cooled slightly, transfer it to a heatproof jar or container. Allow it to cool completely before storing it in the refrigerator for up to 30 days.

Red Sauce Pizzas

The smoky flavors of plank grilling have made their way into every one of these delicious red sauce pizzas. The natural sweetness of tomatoes is concentrated and enhanced by wafting woodsmoke, which delicately flavors every ingredient it touches. It gives the pizzas in this chapter a deep complexity that you can't get with traditionally baked pizzas.

Most of the pizzas in this chapter start with Crushed Tomato Sauce (page 29), made from crushed tomatoes, garlic, olive oil, salt, and pepper, as the base. With a few additional ingredients, however, that simple sauce can become a marinara, a tomato-pomegranate sauce, an Indian-style butter chicken sauce, or other delicious variants. Matching the sauces with the perfect toppings results in mouthwatering flavor combinations.

Four Cheese Pizza

A drizzle of Hot Honey (page 34) right off the grill takes this pizza to the next level. While you don't have to use this combination of cheeses, or even all four of them, they really sing when all melted together. **Serves 4**

1   At least 1 hour before grilling, soak your plank as directed on page 7.

2   Toss together the mozzarella, Fontina, Gruyère, oregano, salt, and pepper in a large bowl. Set aside.

3   Mix the tomato sauce, vinegar, and basil in a medium bowl. Set aside.

4   Flour your work surface well. Stretch the dough with your hands as thinly as possible into a rectangle slightly larger than the plank. As you stretch the dough, move it around to prevent sticking. If the dough is springing back, let it rest for a few minutes, then resume stretching.

5   Preheat the grill and then the plank, and gather your equipment, as directed on page 15.

6   Dust the prepared plank with cornmeal. Fold the pizza dough into thirds and carry it to the grill. Unroll the dough onto the prepared plank, folding up the edges so that the dough is the same size as the plank. Prick the dough all over with a fork, close the lid, and grill for 5 to 7 minutes, until the crust is lightly browned and crisp.

7   Open the grill lid and spread the tomato sauce mixture evenly over the crust. Sprinkle with the cheese mixture. Close the lid and grill until the cheese is golden and bubbly, 5 to 7 minutes. Transfer the pizza to a clean work surface and sprinkle with the Parmesan while it's hot. Let cool for 10 minutes. Drizzle with the Hot Honey, slice, and serve.

½ cup shredded low-moisture mozzarella

½ cup shredded Fontina

½ cup shredded Gruyère

1 teaspoon dried oregano

¼ teaspoon kosher salt (see box, page 25)

¼ teaspoon freshly ground black pepper

1 cup Crushed Tomato Sauce (page 29)

½ teaspoon balsamic vinegar

2 large fresh basil leaves, torn

All-purpose flour

8 to 9 ounces pizza dough, preferably Neapolitan-Style Dough (page 22), at room temperature

Coarse cornmeal

2 tablespoons freshly grated Parmesan

2 tablespoons Hot Honey (page 34) or store-bought hot honey

MAKE IT YOUR OWN
Use regular honey if hot honey is too spicy.

Pizza Margherita

The sauce for this pizza is the Crushed Tomato Sauce (page 29) mixed with a little balsamic vinegar and some torn fresh basil. The balsamic vinegar lightens and smooths out the sauce, and the basil adds some fresh, punchy brightness. **Serves 4**

1 cup Crushed Tomato Sauce (page 29)

½ teaspoon balsamic vinegar

4 large fresh basil leaves, torn

All-purpose flour

8 to 9 ounces pizza dough, preferably Neapolitan-Style Dough (page 22), at room temperature

Coarse cornmeal

8 ounces fresh mozzarella, torn into chunks or sliced

2 tablespoons freshly grated Parmesan

1 At least 1 hour before grilling, soak your plank as directed on page 7.

2 Mix the tomato sauce with the vinegar and half of the basil in a medium bowl. Set aside.

3 Flour your work surface well. Stretch the dough with your hands as thinly as possible into a rectangle slightly larger than the plank. As you stretch the dough, move it around to prevent sticking. If the dough is springing back, let it rest for a few minutes, then resume stretching.

4 Preheat the grill and then the plank, and gather your equipment, as directed on page 15.

5 Dust the prepared plank with cornmeal. Fold the pizza dough into thirds and carry it to the grill. Unroll the dough onto the prepared plank, folding up the edges so that the dough is the same size as the plank. Prick the dough all over with a fork, close the lid, and grill for 5 to 7 minutes, until the crust is lightly browned and crisp.

6 Open the grill lid and spread the tomato sauce mixture evenly over the crust. Top with the mozzarella. Close the lid and grill until the cheese is melted and bubbly, 5 to 7 minutes. Transfer the pizza to a clean work surface, sprinkle with the Parmesan, and let cool for 10 minutes. Sprinkle with the remaining basil, slice, and serve.

Shakshuka Pizza

An aromatically spiced sauce with gooey mozzarella and deliciously oozing egg yolk makes this pizza as flavorful as it is hearty. **Serves 4**

1 At least 1 hour before grilling, soak your plank as directed on page 7.

2 Heat the oil in a large skillet over medium-high heat. Add the onion and jalapeño and sauté until the vegetables have softened, 2 to 3 minutes. Add the cumin and salt, then cook an additional 30 seconds. Stir in the tomato sauce, harissa, and sugar, then lower the heat and cook until the mixture thickens slightly, about 1 minute. Set aside.

3 Flour your work surface well. Stretch the dough with your hands as thinly as possible into a rectangle slightly larger than the plank. As you stretch the dough, move it around to prevent sticking. If the dough is springing back, let it rest for a few minutes, then resume stretching.

4 Preheat the grill and then the plank, and gather your equipment, as directed on page 15.

5 Dust the prepared plank with cornmeal. Fold the pizza dough into thirds and carry it to the grill. Unroll the dough onto the prepared plank, folding up the edges so that the dough is the same size as the plank. Prick the dough all over with a fork, close the lid, and grill for 5 to 7 minutes, until the crust is lightly browned and crisp.

(continues)

1 tablespoon extra virgin olive oil

½ medium onion, chopped

1 jalapeño, seeded and finely chopped (see box, page 44)

½ teaspoon ground cumin

¼ teaspoon kosher salt (see box, page 25)

1 cup Crushed Tomato Sauce (page 29)

1 teaspoon harissa paste

1 teaspoon sugar

All-purpose flour

8 to 9 ounces pizza dough, preferably New York–Style Dough (page 24), at room temperature

Coarse cornmeal

2 cups shredded low-moisture mozzarella

3 large eggs

⅔ cup crumbled feta

¼ cup chopped fresh flat-leaf parsley

MAKE IT AHEAD
The shakshuka sauce can be prepared a day in advance.

6 Open the grill lid and spread the shakshuka sauce evenly over the crust. Sprinkle with the mozzarella, then create three wells on top of the pizza. Gently crack an egg into each well, then sprinkle the feta over the entire pizza. Close the lid and grill until the mozzarella is golden and bubbly and the eggs are cooked over easy, 8 to 9 minutes. Transfer the pizza to a clean work surface and let cool for 10 minutes. Sprinkle with the parsley, slice, and serve.

HOW TO SEED A CHILE

Start by wearing a disposable glove on the hand that touches the chile, so the capsaicin doesn't irritate your skin. Twist the stem to remove, then slice down the middle of the pepper, cutting it in half. Using a spoon, scoop out the seeds and membranes in an upward motion, from the bottom of the chile to the stem (scooping downward tends to clump the seeds at the base of the chile half). If you want some heat, leave a few seeds and a little membrane in the chile—the more you leave, the spicier it will be. Dice the chile by slicing the halves into strips, then cutting them crosswise into small pieces.

Tomato Jam, Goat Cheese, and Pepperoni Pizza

This planked pizza hits all the right notes: sweet tomato jam, spicy pepperoni, tangy goat cheese, and peppery arugula. On top of a smoky artisanal crust, it's perfection. Try the sweet tomato jam on burgers, too. **Serves 4**

1 At least 1 hour before grilling, soak your plank as directed on page 7.

2 Bring the tomatoes, brown sugar, rosemary, ½ teaspoon of salt, ¼ teaspoon of black pepper, the red pepper flakes, and ginger to a boil in a medium saucepan over medium-high heat. Reduce the heat to medium and continue cooking, stirring occasionally, until the tomatoes break down and resembles jam, 25 to 30 minutes. Set aside.

3 Flour your work surface well. Stretch the dough with your hands as thinly as possible into a rectangle slightly larger than the plank. As you stretch the dough, move it around to prevent sticking. If the dough is springing back, let it rest for a few minutes, then resume stretching.

4 Preheat the grill and then the plank, and gather your equipment, as directed on page 15.

5 Dust the prepared plank with cornmeal. Fold the pizza dough into thirds and carry it to the grill. Unroll the dough onto the prepared plank, folding up the edges so that the dough is the same size as the plank. Prick the dough all over with a fork, close the lid, and grill for 5 to 7 minutes, until the crust is lightly browned and crisp.

(continues)

1 pound tomatoes, cored and chopped

¼ cup packed light brown sugar

1 tablespoon fresh rosemary, finely chopped

½ teaspoon kosher salt (see box, page 25), plus more as needed

¼ teaspoon freshly ground black pepper, plus more as needed

¼ teaspoon red pepper flakes

¼ teaspoon ground ginger

All-purpose flour

8 to 9 ounces pizza dough, preferably New York–Style Dough (page 24), at room temperature

Coarse cornmeal

2 cups shredded low-moisture mozzarella

10 pepperoni slices

1 cup crumbled goat cheese

1 cup loosely packed arugula

1 teaspoon extra virgin olive oil

1 teaspoon balsamic vinegar

6 Open the grill lid and spread the tomato jam evenly over the crust. Sprinkle with the mozzarella, then top with the pepperoni and goat cheese. Close the lid and grill until the cheese is golden and bubbly, 5 to 7 minutes. Transfer the pizza to a clean work surface and let cool for 10 minutes.

7 In a medium bowl, combine the arugula, oil, and vinegar and toss. Season to taste with salt and black pepper. Top the pizza with the arugula salad, slice, and serve.

MAKE IT AHEAD
The tomato jam can be prepared up to 3 days ahead.

Barbecued Brisket Pizza

Leftover brisket (or rotisserie chicken) can easily be converted into a sensational pizza when combined with barbecue sauce, oozing cheese, and woodsmoke. If you don't feel like making your own barbecue sauce, use your favorite store-bought sauce. **Serves 4**

1   At least 1 hour before grilling, soak your plank as directed on page 7.

2   Whisk together the tomato sauce, vinegar, brown sugar, molasses, Worcestershire sauce, paprika, dry mustard, onion powder, garlic powder, and cayenne in a medium saucepan over medium heat. Bring to a boil, then reduce the heat to low and simmer, uncovered, for about 15 minutes, or until the sauce thickens. Set aside.

3   Toss the brisket with ⅓ cup of the barbecue sauce.

4   Flour your work surface well. Stretch the dough with your hands as thinly as possible into a rectangle slightly larger than the plank. As you stretch the dough, move it around to prevent sticking. If the dough is springing back, let it rest for a few minutes, then resume stretching.

5   Preheat the grill and then the plank, and gather your equipment, as directed on page 15.

6   Dust the prepared plank with cornmeal. Fold the pizza dough into thirds and carry it to the grill. Unroll the dough onto the prepared plank, folding up the edges so that the dough is the same size as the plank. Prick the dough all over with a fork, close the lid, and grill for 5 to 7 minutes, until the crust is lightly browned and crisp.

(continues)

---

1 cup Crushed Tomato Sauce (page 29)

¼ cup apple cider vinegar

3 tablespoons light brown sugar

2 tablespoons molasses

1½ tablespoons Worcestershire sauce

1 teaspoon paprika

½ teaspoon dry mustard

½ teaspoon onion powder

½ teaspoon garlic powder

⅛ teaspoon cayenne

1½ cups cooked shredded brisket (see Note, page 50)

All-purpose flour

8 to 9 ounces pizza dough, preferably Beer Pizza Dough (page 26), at room temperature

Coarse cornmeal

1 cup shredded low-moisture mozzarella

1 cup shredded Cheddar

1 small tomato, sliced

⅓ cup sliced red onion

¼ cup pickled jalapeño slices (optional)

7 Open the grill lid and spread the remaining barbecue sauce evenly over the crust. Sprinkle with the mozzarella and Cheddar, add the tomato, then top with the brisket, onion, and jalapeño, if desired. Close the lid and grill until the cheese is golden and bubbly, 5 to 7 minutes. Transfer the pizza to a clean work surface and let cool for 10 minutes. Slice and serve.

Note: *This is an excellent use of any leftover cooked brisket. Simply shred the meat with two forks.*

MAKE IT YOUR OWN

Substitute leftover chicken, pork, or beef prepared another way for the brisket.

MAKE IT AHEAD

The barbecue sauce can be prepared up to 3 days in advance.

Meatball and Tomato Pomegranate Pizza

The slightly sweet, slightly tangy tomato pomegranate sauce and spiced meatballs make a winning combination. My suggestion: Pair this pizza with a delicious porter or other dark beer. **Serves 4**

1 At least 1 hour before grilling, soak your plank as directed on page 7.

2 Preheat the oven to 375°F.

3 Combine the panko, egg, garlic, oil, salt, ¼ teaspoon of allspice, ¼ teaspoon of cinnamon, the cumin, onion powder, garlic powder, pepper, and water in a bowl and mix well. Let the mixture sit 5 minutes to hydrate. Add the ground beef and combine very gently with a fork. Using your hands, gently form the mixture into 1½-inch meatballs. You will have 10 to 12 meatballs. Place the meatballs on a baking sheet and bake for 15 minutes. Remove meatballs from the oven and let rest for 30 minutes. Halve the meatballs and set aside.

4 Stir together the tomato sauce, molasses, honey, oregano, the remaining ¼ teaspoon of allspice, and the remaining ¼ teaspoon of cinnamon in a medium bowl. Set aside.

5 Flour your work surface well. Stretch the dough with your hands as thinly as possible into a rectangle slightly larger than the plank. As you stretch the dough, move it around to prevent sticking. If the dough is springing back, let it rest for a few minutes, then resume stretching.

(continues)

½ cup panko bread crumbs

1 large egg, beaten

2 garlic cloves, minced

1 tablespoon extra virgin olive oil

½ teaspoon kosher salt (see box, page 25)

½ teaspoon ground allspice

½ teaspoon ground cinnamon

¼ teaspoon ground cumin

¼ teaspoon onion powder

¼ teaspoon garlic powder

¼ teaspoon freshly ground black pepper

2 tablespoons water

8 ounces ground beef or lamb

1 cup Crushed Tomato Sauce (page 29)

2 tablespoons pomegranate molasses (page 52)

1 tablespoon honey

¼ teaspoon dried oregano

All-purpose flour

(ingredients continue)

6 Preheat the grill and then the plank, and gather your equipment, as directed on page 15.

7 Dust the prepared plank with cornmeal. Fold the pizza dough into thirds and carry it to the grill. Unroll the dough onto the prepared plank, folding up the edges so that the dough is the same size as the plank. Prick the dough all over with a fork, close the lid, and grill for 5 to 7 minutes, until the crust is lightly browned and crisp.

8 Open the grill lid and spread the sauce evenly over the crust. Sprinkle with half of the Fontina, add the meatballs, then top with the remaining Fontina. Close the lid and grill until the cheese is hot and bubbly, 5 to 7 minutes. Transfer the pizza to a clean work surface and let cool for 10 minutes. Sprinkle with the mint, slice, and serve.

Note: *There was a time when I could find pomegranate molasses only in Middle Eastern stores, but these days it's sold at many grocery stores, including Walmart, Trader Joe's, and Whole Foods.*

8 to 9 ounces pizza dough, preferably the Beer Pizza Dough (page 26), at room temperature

Coarse cornmeal

2 cups shredded Fontina

¼ cup coarsely chopped fresh mint

MAKE IT YOUR OWN

Swap out the panko bread crumbs for oats, bulgur, or standard bread crumbs. Or try different cheeses such as Cheddar or Gouda.

MAKE IT AHEAD

Cook the meatballs and sauce 1 to 2 days ahead— just bring them to room temperature before you grill the pizza.

Pizza with Steak and Mole Sauce

Inspired by a mole rub I use when grilling steaks, this pizza sauce is infused with chile powder, cocoa, cinnamon, and other spices, yielding the most delicious foil for a crunchy crust and melty Monterey Jack. **Serves 4**

1 At least 1 hour before grilling, soak your plank as directed on page 7.

2 Whisk together the tomato sauce, chile powder, cocoa powder, brown sugar, cinnamon, and cumin in a medium bowl until combined to make the mole sauce.

3 Toss the steak with ¼ cup of the mole sauce in a medium bowl and set aside.

4 Flour your work surface well. Stretch the dough with your hands as thinly as possible into a rectangle slightly larger than the plank. As you stretch the dough, move it around to prevent sticking. If the dough is springing back, let it rest for a few minutes, then resume stretching.

5 Preheat the grill and then the plank, and gather your equipment, as directed on page 15.

6 Dust the prepared plank with cornmeal. Fold the pizza dough into thirds and carry it to the grill. Unroll the dough onto the prepared plank, folding up the edges so that the dough is the same size as the plank. Prick the dough all over with a fork, close the lid, and grill for 5 to 7 minutes, until the crust is lightly browned and crisp.

1 cup Crushed Tomato Sauce (page 29)

1 tablespoon ancho chile powder

½ tablespoon unsweetened cocoa powder

½ tablespoon light brown sugar

1 teaspoon ground cinnamon

½ teaspoon ground cumin

8 ounces cooked steak, thinly sliced and chopped into ½-inch pieces (see Note)

All-purpose flour

8 to 9 ounces pizza dough, preferably New York–Style Dough (page 24), at room temperature

Coarse cornmeal

2 cups shredded Monterey Jack

½ cup fresh or defrosted frozen corn kernels

¼ cup thinly sliced red onion

¼ cup coarsely chopped fresh cilantro

7 Open the grill lid and spread the remaining mole sauce evenly over the crust. Sprinkle with the Monterey Jack, then top with the steak mixture, corn, and onion. Close the lid and grill until the cheese is golden and bubbly, 5 to 7 minutes. Transfer the pizza to a clean work surface and let cool for 10 minutes. Sprinkle with the cilantro, slice, and serve.

Note: *Filet, sirloin, strip, rib eye, flank, or skirt steak all work with this recipe.*

MAKE IT YOUR OWN

Swap out the steak for shredded chicken or pork.

MAKE IT AHEAD

The mole sauce can be made a day in advance. Bring it to room temperature before tossing it with the steak and grilling the pizza.

Chorizo and Sweet Potato Pizza

This recipe calls for Mexican chorizo, a fresh and aromatic sausage that pairs quite well with the sweet potato. If you would rather use a dry-cured sausage, like Spanish chorizo, dice it into ½-inch cubes and brown it in a skillet first. **Serves 4**

1 medium sweet potato (8 ounces), peeled and cut into ½-inch cubes

1 tablespoon extra virgin olive oil

½ teaspoon kosher salt (see box, page 25)

¼ teaspoon freshly ground black pepper

9 ounces fresh Mexican chorizo

All-purpose flour

8 to 9 ounces pizza dough, preferably New York–Style Dough (page 24), at room temperature

Coarse cornmeal

1 cup Crushed Tomato Sauce (page 29)

2 cups shredded Monterey Jack

¼ cup chopped fresh cilantro

2 tablespoons sliced green onion, white and green parts

1 At least 1 hour before grilling, soak your plank as directed on page 7.

2 Preheat the oven to 450°F.

3 Toss the sweet potatoes with the oil, salt, and pepper on a large baking sheet. Roast for 10 to 15 minutes, tossing the pieces halfway through, until tender.

4 While the potatoes are roasting, heat a medium skillet over medium-high heat. Cook the chorizo, breaking it up into small chunks, until cooked through, 7 to 9 minutes. Transfer the chorizo to a paper-towel-lined plate.

5 Flour your work surface well. Stretch the dough with your hands as thinly as possible into a rectangle slightly larger than the plank. As you stretch the dough, move it around to prevent sticking. If the dough is springing back, let it rest for a few minutes, then resume stretching.

6 Preheat the grill and then the plank, and gather your equipment, as directed on page 15.

7 Dust the prepared plank with cornmeal. Fold the pizza dough into thirds and carry it to the grill. Unroll the dough onto the prepared plank, folding up the edges so that the dough is the same size as the plank. Prick the dough all over with a fork, close the lid, and grill for 5 to 7 minutes, until the crust is lightly browned and crisp.

8 Open the grill lid and spread the sauce evenly over the crust. Sprinkle with Monterey Jack, then top with the chorizo and sweet potato. Close the lid and grill until the cheese is golden and bubbly, 5 to 7 minutes. Transfer the pizza to a clean work surface and let cool for 10 minutes. Sprinkle with the cilantro and green onion, slice, and serve.

MAKE IT YOUR OWN
Swap out the sweet potato for russet potato.

Sausage and Fennel Pizza

Subtly sweet, anise-scented fresh fennel plays beautifully with fennel seed–flecked sweet Italian sausage and red sauce—all together they make this pizza a flavor masterpiece. Try to find the Gruyère for topping—it makes a huge difference. **Serves 4**

3 teaspoons extra virgin olive oil

8 ounces sweet Italian sausage, casing removed

½ small fennel bulb, thinly sliced

Kosher salt (see box, page 25)

Freshly ground black pepper

1 cup Crushed Tomato Sauce (page 29)

½ teaspoon balsamic vinegar

4 large fresh basil leaves, torn

All-purpose flour

8 to 9 ounces pizza dough, preferably Beer Pizza Dough (page 26), at room temperature

Coarse cornmeal

2 cups freshly grated Gruyère

1 At least 1 hour before grilling, soak your plank as directed on page 7.

2 Heat 2 teaspoons of oil in a large skillet over medium-high heat. Add the sausage and cook, breaking it up into small chunks, until browned, about 5 minutes. Remove from the skillet and place on a paper-towel-lined plate.

3 Toss together the fennel and the remaining 1 teaspoon of oil in a small bowl; season to taste with salt and pepper.

4 Combine the tomato sauce, vinegar, and half of the basil in a small bowl. Set aside.

5 Flour your work surface well. Stretch the dough with your hands as thinly as possible into a rectangle slightly larger than the plank. As you stretch the dough, move it around to prevent sticking. If the dough is springing back, let it rest for a few minutes, then resume stretching.

6 Preheat the grill and then the plank, and gather your equipment, as directed on page 15.

7 Dust the prepared plank with cornmeal. Fold the pizza dough into thirds and carry it to the grill. Unroll the dough onto the prepared plank, folding up the edges so that the dough is the same size as the plank. Prick the dough all over with a fork, close the lid, and grill for 5 to 7 minutes, until the crust is lightly browned and crisp.

8 Open the grill lid and spread the tomato sauce mixture evenly over the crust. Sprinkle with the Gruyère, then top with the sausage and fennel. Close the lid and grill until the cheese is golden and bubbly, 5 to 7 minutes. Transfer the pizza to a clean work surface and let cool for 10 minutes. Sprinkle with the remaining basil, slice, and serve.

MAKE IT YOUR OWN

Swap out the sweet Italian sausage for a hot Italian sausage if you like things a bit spicier.

Sloppy Joe Pizza

Sometimes simple trumps fancy. Combining the sweet tang of a sloppy joe with wood smoke from the grill makes this pizza the ultimate comfort food. **Serves 4**

1 At least 1 hour before grilling, soak your plank as directed on page 7.

2 Heat the oil in a large skillet over medium-high heat. Add the onion and sauté until softened, about 5 minutes. Add the ground beef and cook until browned, about 3 minutes. Stir in the chili powder, dry mustard, salt, and pepper and cook for 30 seconds. Add the tomato sauce, brown sugar, Worcestershire sauce, and vinegar. Reduce the heat to medium-low and simmer until slightly thickened, 2 to 3 minutes. Set aside.

3 Flour your work surface well. Stretch the dough with your hands as thinly as possible into a rectangle slightly larger than the plank. As you stretch the dough, move it around to prevent sticking. If the dough is springing back, let it rest for a few minutes, then resume stretching.

4 Preheat the grill and then the plank, and gather your equipment, as directed on page 15.

5 Dust the prepared plank with cornmeal. Fold the pizza dough into thirds and carry it to the grill. Unroll the dough onto the prepared plank, folding up the edges so that the dough is the same size as the plank. Prick the dough all over with a fork, close the lid, and grill for 5 to 7 minutes, until the crust is lightly browned and crisp.

6 Open the grill lid and sprinkle the cheese evenly over the crust. Top with the ground beef mixture. Close the lid and grill until the cheese is bubbly, 5 to 7 minutes. Transfer the pizza to a clean work surface and let cool for 10 minutes. Sprinkle with the green onion, slice, and serve.

2 teaspoons extra virgin olive oil

1 small onion, chopped

8 ounces lean ground beef

½ tablespoon chili powder

1 teaspoon dry mustard

½ teaspoon kosher salt (see box, page 25)

¼ teaspoon freshly ground black pepper

1 cup Crushed Tomato Sauce (page 29)

⅓ cup packed light brown sugar

½ tablespoon Worcestershire sauce

½ tablespoon apple cider vinegar

All-purpose flour

8 to 9 ounces pizza dough, preferably Beer Pizza Dough (page 26), at room temperature

Coarse cornmeal

2 cups shredded mozzarella and Cheddar blend

2 tablespoons sliced green onion, white and green parts

Korean Pulled Pork Pizza

One of my all-time favorite pizzas is a pulled pork pizza, and I've been making it for years. It's easy to pull together using leftover roast pork, and everyone loves it. This is a Korean-inspired take on it—the addition of gochujang, a Korean chile paste, adds some flavorful heat. Different brands of gochujang have different heat levels, so start with 2 tablespoons and add more if you prefer a spicier sauce. **Serves 4**

1 At least 1 hour before grilling, soak your plank as directed on page 7.

2 Heat the oil in a medium saucepan over medium-high heat. Add the onion and cook until softened and translucent, 2 to 3 minutes. Add the tomato sauce, brown sugar, gochujang, vinegar, soy sauce, molasses, lime juice, and ginger and bring to a boil. Reduce the heat to low, then simmer for about 5 minutes, until slightly thickened.

3 Toss the shredded pork with ⅓ cup of the sauce mixture in a medium bowl.

4 Flour your work surface well. Stretch the dough with your hands as thinly as possible into a rectangle slightly larger than the plank. As you stretch the dough, move it around to prevent sticking. If the dough is springing back, let it rest for a few minutes, then resume stretching.

5 Preheat the grill and then the plank, and gather your equipment, as directed on page 15.

(continues)

1 tablespoon sesame oil

1 small onion, chopped

1 cup Crushed Tomato Sauce (page 29)

¼ cup packed light brown sugar

2 to 3 tablespoons gochujang

3 tablespoons rice vinegar

2 tablespoons soy sauce

2 tablespoons molasses

2 tablespoons fresh lime juice

1 tablespoon minced fresh ginger

1½ cups shredded cooked pork (see Note, page 62)

All-purpose flour

8 to 9 ounces pizza dough, preferably New York–Style Dough (page 24), at room temperature

Coarse cornmeal

2 cups shredded low-moisture mozzarella

½ cup chopped red bell pepper

¼ cup chopped fresh cilantro

1 teaspoon sesame seeds

6 Dust the prepared plank with cornmeal. Fold the pizza dough into thirds and carry it to the grill. Unroll the dough onto the prepared plank, folding up the edges so that the dough is the same size as the plank. Prick the dough all over with a fork, close the lid, and grill for 5 to 7 minutes, until the crust is lightly browned and crisp.

7 Open the grill lid and spread the remaining sauce evenly over the crust. Sprinkle with the mozzarella, then top with the pork mixture and bell pepper. Close the lid and grill until the cheese is golden and bubbly, 5 to 7 minutes. Transfer the pizza to a clean work surface and let cool for 10 minutes. Sprinkle with the cilantro and sesame seeds, slice, and serve.

Note: *This is an excellent use for any leftover cooked pork. Simply pull the meat from the bone, if any, place it in a bowl, and shred it with two forks.*

MAKE IT YOUR OWN

Substitute shredded chicken or shredded beef. You can also swap out the red bell pepper for other vegetables like mushrooms or corn, or eliminate the veggies altogether.

Moroccan-Inspired Lamb and Apricot Pizza

Lamb and apricot stew is a traditional Moroccan dish made in a tagine, a clay vessel that allows for slow cooking. I bought a tagine years ago, just to make this stew. Converting the intoxicating flavors of the slow-cooked stew to a planked pizza was an act of love. The rich lamb and apricot flavors, together with mildly spicy harissa sauce, meld perfectly over the creamy, nutty Fontina and crispy crust. **Serves 4**

1 At least 1 hour before grilling, soak your plank as directed on page 7.

2 Drain the apricots and thinly slice. Set aside.

3 Combine the tomato sauce and harissa in a medium bowl and stir to combine. Set aside.

4 Heat the oil in a large skillet over medium-high heat. Add the lamb, garlic, coriander, salt, cumin, paprika, cinnamon, garlic powder, ginger, and cayenne and cook until the lamb is no longer pink, about 5 minutes. Set aside.

5 Flour your work surface well. Stretch the dough with your hands as thinly as possible into a rectangle slightly larger than the plank. As you stretch the dough, move it around to prevent sticking. If the dough is springing back, let it rest for a few minutes, then resume stretching.

6 Preheat the grill and then the plank, and gather your equipment, as directed on page 15.

10 dried apricots, soaked in boiling water for 20 minutes

1 cup Crushed Tomato Sauce (page 29)

2 tablespoons harissa paste

2 teaspoons extra virgin olive oil

8 ounces ground lamb

1 garlic clove, minced

½ teaspoon ground coriander

½ teaspoon kosher salt (see box, page 25)

¼ teaspoon ground cumin

¼ teaspoon sweet paprika

¼ teaspoon ground cinnamon

¼ teaspoon garlic powder

¼ teaspoon ground ginger

¼ teaspoon cayenne

All-purpose flour

8 to 9 ounces pizza dough, preferably New York–Style Dough (page 24), at room temperature

Coarse cornmeal

2 cups shredded Fontina

¼ cup chopped fresh cilantro

7 Dust the prepared plank with cornmeal. Fold the pizza dough into thirds and carry it to the grill. Unroll the dough onto the prepared plank, folding up the edges so that the dough is the same size as the plank. Prick the dough all over with a fork, close the lid, and grill for 5 to 7 minutes, until the crust is lightly browned and crisp.

8 Open the grill lid and spread the tomato-harissa sauce evenly over the crust. Sprinkle with the Fontina, then top with the cooked lamb and sliced apricots. Close the lid and grill until the cheese is hot and bubbly, 5 to 7 minutes. Transfer the pizza to a clean work surface and let cool for 10 minutes. Sprinkle with the cilantro, slice, and serve.

MAKE IT YOUR OWN

Play around with different cheeses such as provolone, pepper jack, Gruyère, Manchego, or Havarti.

Buffalo Chicken Pizza

This smoky, tangy pizza is an excellent way to use store-bought rotisserie chicken or any leftover cooked chicken. Simply pull the meat from the bones and place it in a bowl, then shred it with two forks. **Serves 4**

1 At least 1 hour before grilling, soak your plank as directed on page 7.

2 Combine the tomato sauce, hot sauce, and cream in a medium saucepan over medium-high heat. Cook until slightly thickened, about 10 minutes.

3 Toss the chicken with ¼ cup of the tomato sauce mixture in a medium bowl and set aside.

4 Flour your work surface well. Stretch the dough with your hands as thinly as possible into a rectangle slightly larger than the plank. As you stretch the dough, move it around to prevent sticking. If the dough is springing back, let it rest for a few minutes, then resume stretching.

5 Preheat the grill and then the plank, and gather your equipment, as directed on page 15.

6 Dust the prepared plank with cornmeal. Fold the pizza dough into thirds and carry it to the grill. Unroll the dough onto the prepared plank, folding up the edges so that the dough is the same size as the plank. Prick the dough all over with a fork, close the lid, and grill for 5 to 7 minutes, until the crust is lightly browned and crisp.

7 Open the grill lid and spread the remaining sauce evenly over the crust. Sprinkle with the mozzarella, then top with the chicken mixture and blue cheese. Close the lid and grill until the cheese is golden and bubbly, 5 to 7 minutes. Transfer the pizza to a work surface and let cool slightly. Sprinkle with the green onion, slice, and serve with dressing on the side.

½ cup Crushed Tomato Sauce (page 29)

½ cup hot sauce, preferably Frank's RedHot Original

2 tablespoons heavy cream

1½ cups cooked shredded chicken (see headnote)

All-purpose flour

8 to 9 ounces pizza dough, preferably Beer Pizza Dough (page 26), at room temperature

Coarse cornmeal

2 cups shredded low-moisture mozzarella

4 tablespoons crumbled blue cheese

2 tablespoons sliced green onion, white and green parts

Ranch dressing for serving

MAKE IT AHEAD

The sauce can be prepared up to 3 days in advance. Bring it to room temperature before using.

Butter Chicken Pizza

This Indian-inspired pizza is almost like a marriage of butter chicken and naan—all fired together with wood and topped with gooey mozzarella and crisp onion and pepper. It's absolutely delicious. **Serves 4**

1 At least 1 hour before grilling, soak your plank as directed on page 7.

2 Melt the ghee in a medium skillet over medium-high heat. Add the onion and sauté until translucent and softened, 2 to 3 minutes. Stir in the sugar, chile powder, ginger, garam masala, curry powder, and salt and cook for another 30 seconds, until the sugar dissolves. Add the tomato sauce and vinegar, reduce the heat to medium-low, and simmer for 5 minutes. Stir in the cream and simmer for another 5 minutes. Set aside.

3 Toss the chicken with ⅓ cup of the sauce mixture in a medium bowl and set aside.

4 Flour your work surface well. Stretch the dough with your hands as thinly as possible into a rectangle slightly larger than the plank. As you stretch the dough, move it around to prevent sticking. If the dough is springing back, let it rest for a few minutes, then resume stretching.

5 Preheat the grill and then the plank, and gather your equipment, as directed on page 15.

6 Dust the prepared plank with cornmeal. Fold the pizza dough into thirds and carry it to the grill. Unroll the dough onto the prepared plank, folding up the edges so that the dough is the same size as the plank. Prick the dough all over with a fork, close the lid, and grill for 5 to 7 minutes, until the crust is lightly browned and crisp.

2 tablespoons ghee or butter

¾ cup chopped onion

¼ cup sugar

2 tablespoons Kashmiri chile powder (see Note)

1 tablespoon minced fresh ginger

1 teaspoon garam masala

½ teaspoon curry powder

½ teaspoon kosher salt (see box, page 25)

1 cup Crushed Tomato Sauce (page 29)

2 tablespoons white vinegar

3 tablespoons heavy cream or full-fat coconut milk

1½ cups cooked shredded chicken

All-purpose flour

8 to 9 ounces pizza dough, preferably New York–Style Dough (page 24), at room temperature

Coarse cornmeal

2 cups shredded low-moisture mozzarella

⅓ cup chopped red bell pepper

⅓ cup chopped red onion

¼ cup chopped fresh cilantro

7   Open the grill lid and spread the remaining sauce
    evenly over the crust. Sprinkle with the mozzarella,
    then top with the chicken mixture, bell pepper, and
    onion. Close the lid and grill until the cheese is golden
    and bubbly, 5 to 7 minutes. Transfer the pizza to
    a clean work surface and let cool for 10 minutes.
    Sprinkle with the cilantro, slice, and serve.

Note: *Kashmiri chile powder has slightly more heat
than paprika. If you can't find it, feel free to substitute
paprika, and if you like things spicier, add a pinch of
ground cayenne.*

MAKE IT AHEAD
You can prepare the sauce
a day ahead—just bring
it to room temperature
before grilling the pizza.

Peking Duck Pizza

My love for hoisin sauce—that tangy, sweet sauce that's served with Peking duck—inspired this recipe. It's even more delicious on a pizza. And take note: Cooking the duck breast in a cold pan yields the crispiest skin ever (try this genius technique with chicken thighs, too!).

Serves 4

1 At least 1 hour before grilling, soak your plank as directed on page 7.

2 Season the duck with the salt, pepper, and ¼ teaspoon of five-spice powder. Cut several slits into the fatty skin of the duck breast and then place the duck breast, fat side down, in a large, cold skillet. Heat over medium heat for 6 to 7 minutes, until the skin is crisp. Reduce the heat to low, flip the duck to skin side up, and continue to cook for an additional 10 minutes for medium-rare. Transfer the duck, skin side up, to a cutting board and let rest for 5 minutes. Cut the duck into ½-inch cubes and set aside.

3 Mix the tomato sauce, hoisin sauce, and the remaining ¼ teaspoon of five-spice powder in a medium bowl until combined.

4 Toss 2 tablespoons of the tomato sauce mixture with the duck in a medium bowl. Set aside.

5 Flour your work surface well. Stretch the dough with your hands as thinly as possible into a rectangle slightly larger than the plank. As you stretch the dough, move it around to prevent sticking. If the dough is springing back, let it rest for a few minutes, then resume stretching.

(continues)

1 (8-ounce) boneless, skin-on duck breast half

¼ teaspoon kosher salt (see box, page 25)

¼ teaspoon freshly ground black pepper

½ teaspoon five-spice powder

1 cup Crushed Tomato Sauce (page 29)

¼ cup hoisin sauce

All-purpose flour

8 to 9 ounces pizza dough, preferably New York–Style Dough (page 24), at room temperature

Coarse cornmeal

2 cups shredded Monterey Jack

½ cup chopped red bell pepper

2 tablespoons sliced green onion, white and green parts

¼ cup chopped fresh cilantro

1 teaspoon sesame seeds

6 Preheat the grill and then the plank, and gather your equipment, as directed on page 15.

7 Dust the prepared plank with cornmeal. Fold the pizza dough into thirds and carry it to the grill. Unroll the dough onto the prepared plank, folding up the edges so that the dough is the same size as the plank. Prick the dough all over with a fork, close the lid and grill for 5 to 7 minutes, until the crust is lightly browned and crisp.

8 Open the grill lid and spread the remaining tomato sauce mixture evenly over the crust. Sprinkle with the Monterey Jack, then top with the duck and bell pepper. Close the lid and grill until the cheese is melted and bubbly, 5 to 7 minutes. Transfer the pizza to a clean work surface and let cool for 10 minutes. Sprinkle with the green onion, cilantro, and sesame seeds, slice, and serve.

MAKE IT YOUR OWN

Substitute a chicken thigh or 1½ cups of shredded rotisserie chicken for the duck breast. Try different vegetables on this pizza, like mushrooms, red onions, and snow peas.

Shrimp Fra Diavolo Pizza

A pizza sauce inspired by fra diavolo, a spicy tomato sauce typically served with seafood and pasta, helps create the perfect base for this pizza. Try to find large shrimp for this recipe so they stay moist while being grilled. **Serves 4**

1   At least 1 hour before grilling, soak your plank as directed on page 7.

2   Season the shrimp with ½ teaspoon of salt and ¼ teaspoon of black pepper. Heat 1 tablespoon of oil in a large skillet over medium-high heat. Add the shrimp and cook for 1 minute on each side. Transfer the shrimp to a cutting board and cut into ½-inch pieces. (The shrimp will not be cooked through yet, so don't worry if they still look somewhat gray and translucent.)

3   Add the remaining 2 tablespoons of oil to the skillet. Add the onion and sauté on medium-high heat for about 5 minutes, or until softened and translucent. Add the garlic, red pepper flakes, oregano, the remaining ½ teaspoon of salt, and the remaining ¼ teaspoon of black pepper and sauté for 30 seconds. Add the wine and deglaze the pan by gently scraping up any pieces of food stuck to the bottom of the skillet. Add the tomatoes, reduce the heat to medium-low, and simmer for 12 to 15 minutes, stirring occasionally, until most of the liquid has evaporated and the mixture slightly thickens and becomes saucy. Remove from the heat and set aside.

(continues)

8 ounces large shrimp, shelled and deveined

1 teaspoon kosher salt (see box, page 25)

½ teaspoon freshly ground black pepper

3 tablespoons extra virgin olive oil

1 small onion, thinly sliced

3 garlic cloves, minced

½ teaspoon red pepper flakes

½ teaspoon dried oregano

¾ cup white wine

1½ cups grape tomatoes, halved

All-purpose flour

8 to 9 ounces pizza dough, preferably New York–Style Dough (page 24), at room temperature

Coarse cornmeal

2 cups shredded low-moisture mozzarella

2 to 3 large fresh basil leaves, torn

4 Flour your work surface well. Stretch the dough with your hands as thinly as possible into a rectangle slightly larger than the plank. As you stretch the dough, move it around to prevent sticking. If the dough is springing back, let it rest for a few minutes, then resume stretching.

5 Preheat the grill and then the plank, and gather your equipment, as directed on page 15.

6 Dust the prepared plank with cornmeal. Fold the pizza dough into thirds and carry it to the grill. Unroll the dough onto the prepared plank, folding up the edges so that the dough is the same size as the plank. Prick the dough all over with a fork, close the lid, and grill for 5 to 7 minutes, until the crust is lightly browned and crisp.

7 Open the grill lid and sprinkle the mozzarella over the crust, then top with the tomato mixture and shrimp. Close the lid and grill until the cheese is golden and bubbly and the shrimp is cooked through, 5 to 7 minutes. Transfer the pizza to a clean work surface and let cool for 10 minutes. Sprinkle with the basil, slice, and serve.

MAKE IT YOUR OWN

Instead of red pepper flakes, use Calabrian chile paste for a more authentic sauce. You can also substitute other seafood options, like chunks of fish (halibut, cod, snapper, or bass would work great) or lobster for the shrimp.

White Sauce & Green Sauce Pizzas

There's something magical and irresistible about the pizzas in this chapter.

The flavor of the rich Garlic Cream Sauce (page 30), already delicious on its own, is made deeper when introduced to smoke from the grilling plank. These extra creamy pizzas really pack a punch when combined with toppings like dill pickles (I know, I know—sounds weird, but you must try it!), mushrooms and Fontina, spinach and feta, or jerk chicken with rum glaze. The white sauce pizzas in this chapter are some of my favorites.

Green sauce pizzas, on the other hand, hold the honor of having initiated my love of pizza. I grew up in a Middle Eastern household where pizza was a dish called manakeesh, a flatbread covered in a sauce made of za'atar and extra virgin olive oil. I made the green sauce pizzas in this chapter with the more common—and equally flavorful—pesto sauce. With classic ingredients like fresh basil, garlic, Parmesan, pine nuts, lemon juice, and olive oil, my Pesto Sauce (page 33) coaxes new flavors out of favorite toppings like andouille, artichokes, and sun-dried tomatoes.

Crispy Brussels Sprouts and Roasted Tomato Pizza

WITH GARLIC CREAM SAUCE AND BALSAMIC GLAZE

The charred Brussels sprouts lend a mildly sweet and nutty flavor to this veg-forward pie, and roasting the tomatoes beforehand brings out their sweetness and reduces their moisture, ensuring your crust stays crunchy. **Serves 4**

1 At least 1 hour before grilling, soak your plank as directed on page 7.

2 Preheat the oven to 425°F.

3 Place the tomatoes and herbs on a baking sheet, drizzle with 3 tablespoons of oil, ½ teaspoon of salt, and ¼ teaspoon of pepper. Toss to combine, then roast for about 25 minutes, until the tomatoes begin to burst. Discard the herbs and set the tomatoes aside.

4 Toss the sprouts with the remaining 1 tablespoon of oil, ½ teaspoon of salt, and ¼ teaspoon of pepper. Set aside.

5 Flour your work surface well. Stretch the dough with your hands as thinly as possible into a rectangle slightly larger than the plank. As you stretch the dough, move it around to prevent sticking. If the dough is springing back, let it rest for a few minutes, then resume stretching.

6 Preheat the grill and then the plank, and gather your equipment, as directed on page 15.

(continues)

1 pint grape or cherry tomatoes

3 to 4 fresh herb sprigs such as oregano, thyme, or rosemary

4 tablespoons extra virgin olive oil

1 teaspoon kosher salt (see box, page 25)

½ teaspoon freshly ground black pepper

1½ cups Brussels sprouts, trimmed and thinly sliced

All-purpose flour

8 to 9 ounces pizza dough, preferably New York–Style Dough (page 24), at room temperature

Coarse cornmeal

1 cup Garlic Cream Sauce (page 30)

1 cup shredded low-moisture mozzarella

2 tablespoons Balsamic Glaze (page 35)

7 Dust the prepared plank with cornmeal. Fold the pizza dough into thirds and carry it to the grill. Unroll the dough onto the prepared plank, folding up the edges so that the dough is the same size as the plank. Prick the dough all over with a fork, close the lid, and grill for 5 to 7 minutes, until the crust is lightly browned and crisp.

8 Open the grill lid and spread the cream sauce evenly over the crust. Sprinkle with the mozzarella, then top with the sprouts and roasted tomatoes. Close the lid and grill until the cheese is golden and bubbly and the sprouts are slightly charred, 5 to 7 minutes. Transfer the pizza to a clean work surface and let cool for 10 minutes. Drizzle with the balsamic glaze, slice, and serve.

Pickle Pizza

WITH GARLIC CREAM SAUCE

QC Pizza of Mahtomedi, Minnesota, went viral with its pickle pizza, Kinda Big Dill. It features a garlic dill sauce, Canadian bacon, mozzarella, and lots of sliced pickles. Don't knock it till you've tried it—this pizza is *good*! Here is my take. All inhibitions disappear, as does the pizza itself, when this is on the menu. **Serves 4**

All-purpose flour

8 to 9 ounces pizza dough, preferably Neapolitan-Style Dough (page 22), at room temperature

Coarse cornmeal

1 cup Garlic Cream Sauce (page 30)

1 cup shredded low-moisture mozzarella

1 cup sliced dill pickles

¼ cup (½ ounce) freshly grated Parmesan

1   At least 1 hour before grilling, soak your plank as directed on page 7.

2   Flour your work surface well. Stretch the dough with your hands as thinly as possible into a rectangle slightly larger than the plank. As you stretch the dough, move it around to prevent sticking. If the dough is springing back, let it rest for a few minutes, then resume stretching.

3   Preheat the grill and then the plank, and gather your equipment, as directed on page 15.

4   Dust the prepared plank with cornmeal. Fold the pizza dough into thirds and carry it to the grill. Unroll the dough onto the prepared plank, folding up the edges so that the dough is the same size as the plank. Prick the dough all over with a fork, close the lid, and grill for 5 to 7 minutes, until the crust is lightly browned and crisp.

5   Open the grill lid and spread the cream sauce evenly over the crust. Sprinkle with the mozzarella, then top with the pickle slices. Close the lid and grill until the cheese is golden and bubbly and the pickles are warmed through, 5 to 7 minutes. Transfer the pizza to a clean work surface, sprinkle with the Parmesan, and let cool for 10 minutes. Slice and serve.

Elote Pizza

WITH GARLIC CREAM SAUCE

This pizza recreates my go-to dish when corn is in season: Elote, a Mexican street food staple of grilled corn on the cob slathered in a spicy cream sauce topped with salty cotija cheese and lime juice. **Serves 4**

1   At least 1 hour before grilling, soak your plank as directed on page 7.

2   Heat the oil in a large cast-iron skillet over high heat. Add the corn, salt, chipotle powder, and cumin and stir to combine. Cook without stirring until the corn is lightly charred on one side, about 2 minutes. Toss the corn and repeat until the mixture appears slightly more charred over all, about 2 minutes more. Continue tossing and stirring until the corn is charred all over, 7 to 8 minutes total. Set aside.

3   Flour your work surface well. Stretch the dough with your hands as thinly as possible into a rectangle slightly larger than the plank. As you stretch the dough, move it around to prevent sticking. If the dough is springing back, let it rest for a few minutes, then resume stretching.

4   Preheat the grill and then the plank, and gather your equipment, as directed on page 15.

5   Dust the prepared plank with cornmeal. Fold the pizza dough into thirds and carry it to the grill. Unroll the dough onto the prepared plank, folding up the edges so that the dough is the same size as the plank. Prick the dough all over with a fork, close the lid, and grill for 5 to 7 minutes, until the crust is lightly browned and crisp.

1 tablespoon avocado or vegetable oil

1½ cups fresh or defrosted frozen corn kernels

½ teaspoon kosher salt (see box, page 25)

½ teaspoon chipotle powder

¼ teaspoon ground cumin

All-purpose flour

8 to 9 ounces pizza dough, preferably New York–Style Dough (page 24), at room temperature

Coarse cornmeal

1 cup Garlic Cream Sauce (page 30)

1 cup shredded Monterey Jack

⅔ cup crumbled cotija or feta

2 tablespoons sliced green onion, white and green parts

¼ cup chopped fresh cilantro

1 tablespoon fresh lime juice

6 Open the grill lid and spread the cream sauce evenly over the crust. Sprinkle with the Monterey Jack, then top with the corn mixture and cotija. Close the lid and grill until the Monterey Jack is golden and bubbly, 5 to 7 minutes. Transfer the pizza to a clean work surface and let cool for 10 minutes. Sprinkle with the cilantro, green onion, and lime juice, slice, and serve.

MAKE IT AHEAD

The corn mixture can be prepared a day in advance. Bring it to room temperature before grilling your pizza.

Spanakopita Pizza
WITH GARLIC CREAM SAUCE

Spanakopita is a pastry with a filling of spinach and feta wrapped in delicate phyllo dough. Filling and wrapping each pastry takes time—but spreading the ingredients over a crunchy crust is a faster and just-as-delicious option. **Serves 4**

1 At least 1 hour before grilling, soak your plank as directed on page 7.

2 Mix the spinach with the mozzarella, oregano, salt, and pepper in a large bowl.

3 Flour your work surface well. Stretch the dough with your hands as thinly as possible into a rectangle slightly larger than the plank. As you stretch the dough, move it around to prevent sticking. If the dough is springing back, let it rest for a few minutes, then resume stretching.

4 Preheat the grill and then the plank, and gather your equipment, as directed on page 15.

5 Dust the prepared plank with cornmeal. Fold the pizza dough into thirds and carry it to the grill. Unroll the dough onto the prepared plank, folding up the edges so that the dough is the same size as the plank. Prick the dough all over with a fork, close the lid, and grill for 5 to 7 minutes, until the crust is lightly browned and crisp.

6 Open the grill lid and spread the cream sauce evenly over the crust. Top with the spinach mixture and feta. Close the lid and grill until the mozzarella is golden and bubbly, 5 to 7 minutes. Transfer the pizza to a clean work surface and let cool for 10 minutes. Sprinkle with the green onion, slice, and serve.

8 ounces frozen spinach, thawed and squeezed as dry as possible (to yield about 1 cup spinach)

1¼ cups shredded low-moisture mozzarella

1 tablespoon chopped fresh oregano, or 1 teaspoon dried oregano

½ teaspoon kosher salt (see box, page 25)

¼ teaspoon freshly ground black pepper

All-purpose flour

8 to 9 ounces pizza dough, preferably New York–Style Dough (page 24), at room temperature

Coarse cornmeal

1 cup Garlic Cream Sauce (page 30)

⅔ cup crumbled feta

2 tablespoons sliced green onion, white and green parts

Peach and Corn Pizza

WITH GARLIC CREAM SAUCE

The smoke and wood from the grilling plank really complement the sweetness of the corn and peaches. Coupled with the garlic cream sauce, this is one of the most mouthwatering pizzas. **Serves 4**

1   At least 1 hour before grilling, soak your plank as directed on page 7.

2   Flour your work surface well. Stretch the dough with your hands as thinly as possible into a rectangle slightly larger than the plank. As you stretch the dough, move it around to prevent sticking. If the dough is springing back, let it rest for a few minutes, then resume stretching.

3   Preheat the grill and then the plank, and gather your equipment, as directed on page 15.

4   Dust the prepared plank with cornmeal. Fold the pizza dough into thirds and carry it to the grill. Unroll the dough onto the prepared plank, folding up the edges so that the dough is the same size as the plank. Prick the dough all over with a fork, close the lid, and grill for 5 to 7 minutes, until the crust is lightly browned and crisp.

5   Open the grill lid and spread the cream sauce evenly over the crust. Top with the mozzarella, corn, and peaches. Close the lid and grill until the cheese is golden and bubbly, 5 to 7 minutes. Transfer the pizza to a clean work surface and let cool for 10 minutes. Sprinkle with the basil, drizzle with the balsamic glaze, slice, and serve.

All-purpose flour

8 to 9 ounces pizza dough, preferably New York–Style Dough (page 24), at room temperature

Coarse cornmeal

1 cup Garlic Cream Sauce (page 30)

1 cup shredded low-moisture mozzarella

¾ cup fresh or defrosted frozen corn kernels

¾ cup diced peaches

¼ cup packed fresh basil leaves, sliced in a chiffonade (see Note)

2 tablespoons Balsamic Glaze (page 35)

Note: *To chiffonade basil, stack the leaves one on top of another, roll them up like a cigar, and slice across the roll using a sharp knife. When the basil unrolls, it will look like thin ribbons that are perfect for garnishing.*

Asparagus, Potato, Goat Cheese, and Roasted Tomato Pizza

WITH PESTO SAUCE

This super-easy vegetarian pizza is packed with flavors and textures. If you want to up the protein, add some tofu or chicken, but reduce the quantity of vegetables so your pizza doesn't become too heavy. **Serves 4**

1 At least 1 hour before grilling, soak your plank as directed on page 7.

2 Preheat the oven to 425°F.

3 Place the potato, tomatoes, and asparagus on a baking sheet, drizzle with the oil, and sprinkle with the salt and pepper. Toss the vegetables gently to coat and spread them into a single layer. Roast until the potato and asparagus are tender and golden and the tomatoes are soft, about 20 minutes.

4 Chop the cooked asparagus into ½-inch pieces and transfer them to a large bowl. Add the potato and tomatoes. Add 2 tablespoons of pesto and very gently toss the vegetables. Set them aside.

5 Flour your work surface well. Stretch the dough with your hands as thinly as possible into a rectangle slightly larger than the plank. As you stretch the dough, move it around to prevent sticking. If the dough is springing back, let it rest for a few minutes, then resume stretching.

(continues)

1 small russet potato, cut into ½-inch cubes

1 cup grape or cherry tomatoes

4 to 5 asparagus spears, trimmed

1 tablespoon extra virgin olive oil

1 teaspoon kosher salt (see box, page 25)

½ teaspoon freshly ground black pepper

1 cup Pesto Sauce (page 33) or store-bought pesto

All-purpose flour

8 to 9 ounces pizza dough, preferably Beer Pizza Dough (page 26), at room temperature

Coarse cornmeal

1 cup shredded low-moisture mozzarella

1 cup crumbled goat cheese

6 Preheat the grill and then the plank, and gather your equipment, as directed on page 15.

7 Dust the prepared plank with cornmeal. Fold the pizza dough into thirds and carry it to the grill. Unroll the dough onto the prepared plank, folding up the edges so that the dough is the same size as the plank. Prick the dough all over with a fork, close the lid, and grill for 5 to 7 minutes, until the crust is lightly browned and crisp.

8 Open the grill lid and spread the remaining pesto evenly over the crust. Sprinkle with the mozzarella, then top with the vegetable mixture and goat cheese. Close the lid and grill until the mozzarella is golden and bubbly, 5 to 7 minutes. Transfer the pizza to a clean work surface and let cool for 10 minutes. Slice and serve.

MAKE IT AHEAD
Roast the potato, tomatoes, and asparagus the day before. Bring them to room temperature before tossing them with the pesto and grilling the pizza.

Mushroom and Fontina Pizza
WITH GARLIC CREAM SAUCE

Sautéed mushrooms go great on everything from steak to eggs to pasta. My favorite recipe involves spooning some over toast topped with goat cheese. Here, they combine with Fontina cheese and fragrant Garlic Cream Sauce (page 30) to make this pizza an earthy, elegant, surefire hit. **Serves 4**

1 At least 1 hour before grilling, soak your plank as directed on page 7.

2 Heat a large skillet over medium-high heat. Add the oil and mushrooms and cook without stirring until the mushrooms start to sizzle, about 2 minutes. Add the shallot, garlic, thyme, salt, and pepper and stir to combine. Cook until the shallot has softened, about 1 minute. Stir in the brandy and soy sauce. Continue to cook until the liquid has evaporated, about 30 seconds. Set aside.

3 Flour your work surface well. Stretch the dough with your hands as thinly as possible into a rectangle slightly larger than the plank. As you stretch the dough, move it around to prevent sticking. If the dough is springing back, let it rest for a few minutes, then resume stretching.

4 Preheat the grill and then the plank, and gather your equipment, as directed on page 15.

5 Dust the prepared plank with cornmeal. Fold the pizza dough into thirds and carry it to the grill. Unroll the dough onto the prepared plank, folding up the edges so that the dough is the same size as the plank. Prick the dough all over with a fork, close the lid, and grill for 5 to 7 minutes, until the crust is lightly browned and crisp.

(continues)

1 tablespoon avocado oil
(see Note, page 94)

8 ounces fresh button or cremini mushrooms, cleaned, trimmed, and thinly sliced

1 small shallot, finely chopped

2 garlic cloves, finely chopped

2 teaspoons minced fresh thyme leaves

½ teaspoon kosher salt
(see box, page 25)

¼ teaspoon freshly ground black pepper

2 tablespoons brandy or bourbon

2 teaspoons soy sauce

All-purpose flour

8 to 9 ounces pizza dough, preferably New York–Style Dough (page 24), at room temperature

Coarse cornmeal

1 cup Garlic Cream Sauce (page 30)

1 cup shredded Fontina

2 tablespoons chopped fresh flat-leaf parsley

6   Open the grill lid and spread the cream sauce evenly over the crust. Sprinkle with the Fontina, then top with the mushrooms. Close the lid and grill until the cheese is golden and bubbly, 5 to 7 minutes. Transfer the pizza to a clean work surface and let cool for 10 minutes. Sprinkle with the parsley, slice, and serve.

Note: *I recommend using avocado oil because it has a more neutral taste than olive oil, which tends to be bold, peppery, or fruity. The avocado oil allows the mushrooms to stand out in this pizza.*

MAKE IT YOUR OWN

Try a mix of wild mushrooms on this pizza if they're available—shiitake, oyster, even portobello mushrooms cut into small chunks would be delicious. You can also swap out the thyme for rosemary if you have it on hand. Skip the brandy or bourbon if you don't want the alcohol—it's just as tasty without it.

Cajun Shrimp and Andouille Pizza

WITH PESTO SAUCE

Spicy Cajun shrimp and smoky andouille sausage call up the flavors of my favorite NOLA haunts. A crunchy crust and bubbling mozzarella seal this recipe's place as a total winner. **Serves 4**

1 At least 1 hour before grilling, soak your plank as directed on page 7.

2 Toss the shrimp with the Cajun seasoning in a medium bowl and set aside.

3 Heat the oil in a large skillet over medium-high heat. Add the sausage and cook until browned, about 2 minutes. Transfer the sausage to a paper-towel-lined plate.

4 Add the shrimp to the same skillet and cook for 1 minute on each side. Transfer the shrimp to a cutting board and cut into ½-inch pieces. The shrimp will not be cooked through yet, so don't worry if they still looks somewhat gray and translucent.

5 Flour your work surface well. Stretch the dough with your hands as thinly as possible into a rectangle slightly larger than the plank. As you stretch the dough, move it around to prevent sticking. If the dough is springing back, let it rest for a few minutes, then resume stretching.

6 Preheat the grill and then the plank, and gather your equipment, as directed on page 15.

(continues)

8 ounces large shrimp, peeled and deveined (see Note, page 97)

½ teaspoon Cajun or Creole seasoning

1 teaspoon extra virgin olive oil

6 ounces andouille sausage, cut into ½-inch cubes

All-purpose flour

8 to 9 ounces pizza dough, preferably Beer Pizza Dough (page 26), at room temperature

Coarse cornmeal

1 cup Pesto Sauce (page 33) or store-bought pesto

2 cups shredded low-moisture mozzarella

½ cup chopped red bell pepper

2 tablespoons sliced green onion, white and green parts

7 Dust the prepared plank with cornmeal. Fold the pizza dough into thirds and carry it to the grill. Unroll the dough onto the prepared plank, folding up the edges so that the dough is the same size as the plank. Prick the dough all over with a fork, close the lid, and grill for 5 to 7 minutes, until the crust is lightly browned and crisp.

8 Open the grill lid and spread the pesto evenly over the crust. Sprinkle with the mozzarella, then top with the sausage, shrimp, and bell pepper. Close the lid and grill until the cheese is golden and bubbly, 5 to 7 minutes. Transfer the pizza to a clean work surface and let cool for 10 minutes. Sprinkle with the green onion, slice, and serve.

Note: *Try to find the biggest, plumpest shrimp for this pizza so they stay juicy when they are grilled.*

Chicken, Artichoke, and Sun-Dried Tomato Pizza
WITH PESTO SAUCE

Chicken, artichokes, sun-dried tomatoes, and pesto go so well together, from salads to pastas to sandwiches. I'm probably biased, but on a plank-grilled crust, they taste the best. **Serves 4**

1 At least 1 hour before grilling, soak your plank as directed on page 7.

2 Toss the chicken and sun-dried tomatoes with 2 tablespoons of the pesto in a medium bowl and set aside.

3 Flour your work surface well. Stretch the dough with your hands as thinly as possible into a rectangle slightly larger than the plank. As you stretch the dough, move it around to prevent sticking. If the dough is springing back, let it rest for a few minutes, then resume stretching.

4 Preheat the grill and then the plank, and gather your equipment, as directed on page 15.

5 Dust the prepared plank with cornmeal. Fold the pizza dough into thirds and carry it to the grill. Unroll the dough onto the prepared plank, folding up the edges so that the dough is the same size as the plank. Prick the dough all over with a fork, close the lid, and grill for 5 to 7 minutes, until the crust is lightly browned and crisp.

6 Open the grill lid and spread the remaining pesto evenly over the crust. Sprinkle with the mozzarella, then top with the chicken mixture and artichokes. Close the lid and grill until the cheese is golden and bubbly, 5 to 7 minutes. Transfer the pizza to a clean work surface and let cool for 10 minutes. Slice and serve.

1 cup cooked shredded chicken (see headnote, page 67)

½ cup (8 to 12) sun-dried tomatoes, thinly sliced

1 cup Pesto Sauce (page 33) or store-bought pesto

All-purpose flour

8 to 9 ounces pizza dough, preferably New York–Style Dough (page 24), at room temperature

Coarse cornmeal

2 cups shredded low-moisture mozzarella

¾ cup marinated artichoke hearts, drained and chopped

Jerk Chicken Pizza
WITH GARLIC CREAM SAUCE AND SPICY RUM GLAZE

Don't let the long list of components scare you—most of them can be made ahead of time—and this spicy, fragrant jerk chicken drizzled with rum glaze is definitely worth the effort. **Serves 4**

1 To make the chicken, mix the brown sugar, salt, thyme, black pepper, allspice, garlic powder, cinnamon, cayenne, and oil in a small bowl until well combined. Rub the mixture evenly over the chicken. Refrigerate for 4 hours or up to overnight.

2 At least 1 hour before grilling, soak your plank as directed on page 7.

3 When ready to cook, heat the grill to medium-high heat, 475° to 500°F. Brush the grates with oil and grill the chicken until the internal temperature reaches 165°F, 5 to 6 minutes per side if using chicken thighs, or 4 to 5 minutes per side if using chicken breasts. Let cool, then cut into ½-inch cubes.

4 To make the spicy rum glaze, combine the butter, brown sugar, rum, honey, and cayenne in a small saucepan over medium-high heat and bring to a boil. Reduce the heat to low and simmer for 3 to 4 minutes, until syrupy. Set aside.

5 To make the pizza, flour your work surface well. Stretch the dough with your hands as thinly as possible into a rectangle slightly larger than the plank. As you stretch the dough, move it around to prevent sticking. If the dough is springing back, let it rest for a few minutes, then resume stretching.

For the Chicken

2 teaspoons dark brown sugar

1 teaspoon kosher salt (see box, page 25)

½ teaspoon dried thyme

½ teaspoon freshly ground black pepper

½ teaspoon ground allspice

½ teaspoon garlic powder

¼ teaspoon ground cinnamon

¼ teaspoon cayenne pepper

1 tablespoon extra virgin olive oil, plus more for greasing the grill grates

12 ounces boneless, skinless chicken thighs or breasts

For the Spicy Rum Glaze

2 tablespoons unsalted butter

2 tablespoons dark brown sugar

2 tablespoons rum

2 tablespoons honey

⅛ teaspoon cayenne pepper

6 Preheat the plank as directed on page 7.

7 Dust the prepared plank with cornmeal. Fold the pizza dough into thirds and carry it to the grill. Unroll the dough onto the prepared plank, folding up the edges so that the dough is the same size as the plank. Prick the dough all over with a fork, close the lid, and grill for 5 to 7 minutes, until the crust is lightly browned and crisp.

8 Open the grill lid and spread the cream sauce evenly over the crust. Sprinkle with the mozzarella, then top with the chicken, pineapple, jalapeño, and onion. Close the lid and grill until the cheese is golden and bubbly, 5 to 7 minutes. Transfer the pizza to a clean work surface and let cool for 10 minutes. Drizzle with half of the rum glaze, slice, and serve with the remaining glaze on the side.

MAKE IT AHEAD

The chicken can be made up to 2 days in advance, and the rum glaze can be made up to 3 days in advance—just be sure to warm the glaze in the microwave for 15 seconds before drizzling it on the pizza.

For the Pizza

All-purpose flour

8 to 9 ounces pizza dough, preferably New York–Style Dough (page 24), at room temperature

Coarse cornmeal

1 cup Garlic Cream Sauce (page 30)

1 cup shredded low-moisture mozzarella

½ cup fresh pineapple chunks, cut into ¼-inch cubes

1 tablespoon finely diced jalapeño (seeded, if desired, to reduce heat, see box, page 44)

½ cup chopped red onion

No Sauce Pizzas

This chapter is all about taking the best ingredients available and creating delicious and exciting combinations. I have always gravitated toward pizzas that feature fresh, local, seasonal ingredients and fusions of different international cuisines, and that's what I've provided here. They may sound complicated, but it doesn't get easier than these recipes. Do you have leftover taco meat and veggies? Toss them on a pizza with some cheese for dinner the next day. Do you have fruit or vegetables sitting in your fridge that need to be used? Roast them to bring out their sweetness, mix them with some caramelized onions and cheese, and throw them on a wood plank cradled in chewy, crusty pizza dough.

These are also the pizzas you can serve when entertaining friends who have different flavor preferences. Just visited a farmers market? Make a pizza. Start with the recipes in this chapter, then swap out topping ingredients with those you already have at home.

Pear, Brie, and Caramelized Onion Pizza

Chef Alice Waters taught us that great pizza need not rely on sauce and pepperoni. Seasonal fruits and vegetables—like this combination of pear, Brie, and caramelized onion—can make an outstanding meal. **Serves 4**

1 At least 1 hour before grilling, soak your plank as directed on page 7.

2 Heat 1 tablespoon of oil in a large skillet over medium-high heat. Add the onion, sugar, ½ teaspoon of salt, and the pepper and stir to coat. Cook, stirring occasionally, until the onion begins to soften, about 5 minutes. Reduce the heat to medium-low and cook, stirring frequently, until the onion is caramelized and jammy, about 20 minutes.

3 Combine the remaining 2 tablespoons of oil, the remaining ½ teaspoon of salt, and the herbes de Provence in a small bowl. Set aside.

4 Mix the honey and rosemary in a small microwave-safe bowl. Microwave for 15 seconds. Stir and microwave for another 15 seconds. Set aside.

5 Flour your work surface well. Stretch the dough with your hands as thinly as possible into a rectangle slightly larger than the plank. As you stretch the dough, move it around to prevent sticking. If the dough is springing back, let it rest for a few minutes, then resume stretching.

6 Preheat the grill and then the plank, and gather your equipment, as directed on page 15.

(continues)

3 tablespoons extra virgin olive oil

1 large onion, halved and thinly sliced

1 teaspoon sugar

1 teaspoon kosher salt (see box, page 25)

¼ teaspoon freshly ground black pepper

1 teaspoon herbes de Provence

2 tablespoons honey

1 teaspoon chopped fresh rosemary

All-purpose flour

8 to 9 ounces pizza dough, preferably New York–Style Dough (page 24), at room temperature

Coarse cornmeal

6 ounces Brie, sliced

½ ripe but firm pear, thinly sliced

7   Dust the prepared plank with cornmeal. Fold the pizza dough into thirds and carry it to the grill. Unroll the dough onto the prepared plank, folding up the edges so that the dough is the same size as the plank. Prick the dough all over with a fork, close the lid, and grill for 5 to 7 minutes, until the crust is lightly browned and crisp.

8   Open the grill lid and brush the oil mixture evenly over the crust. Sprinkle with the caramelized onion, then top with the Brie and pear slices. Close the lid and grill until the cheese is melted and bubbly, 5 to 7 minutes. Transfer the pizza to a clean work surface and let cool for 10 minutes. Drizzle with the rosemary honey, slice, and serve.

MAKE IT YOUR OWN

Substitute for other fresh or dried fruit like figs, apricots, peaches, apples, or cranberries for the pear. (If substituting dried fruit, be sure to soak it in a bowl of boiling hot water for 20 minutes. The fruit will be plumper and softer, which makes a real difference in the texture of the pizza.) You can also use other cheeses in place of or in addition to the Brie, like Gorgonzola, Manchego, or Fontina.

Pepperoni and Bacon Jam Pizza

Combining the sweetness of homemade bacon jam, the spiciness of pepperoni, and the creaminess of ricotta makes for an irresistibly delicious pie. **Serves 4**

1 At least 1 hour before grilling, soak your plank as directed on page 7.

2 Cook the bacon in a large skillet over medium heat, stirring occasionally, until the fat has rendered and the bacon has browned, 5 to 7 minutes. Scoop out the bacon and place on a paper-towel-lined plate. Drain all but 2 tablespoons of the bacon fat from the skillet. Add all the bacon back to the skillet, stir in the onion and garlic, and cook until the onion has softened and is translucent, about 5 minutes. Stir in the vinegar, brown sugar, and jalapeños. Simmer uncovered until the liquid turns syrupy and nearly evaporates, 1 to 2 minutes. Set aside.

3 Combine the ricotta and mozzarella in a small bowl and set aside.

4 Flour your work surface well. Stretch the dough with your hands as thinly as possible into a rectangle slightly larger than the plank. As you stretch the dough, move it around to prevent sticking. If the dough is springing back, let it rest for a few minutes, then resume stretching.

5 Preheat the grill and then the plank, and gather your equipment, as directed on page 15.

(continues)

8 ounces bacon, cut into ½-inch pieces

1 small onion, finely chopped

4 garlic cloves, minced

¼ cup balsamic vinegar

¼ cup packed light brown sugar

¼ cup finely chopped pickled jalapeños

½ cup ricotta

1 cup shredded low-moisture mozzarella

All-purpose flour

8 to 9 ounces pizza dough, preferably Beer Pizza Dough (page 26), at room temperature

Coarse cornmeal

10 pepperoni slices

2 tablespoons Hot Honey (page 34) or store-bought hot honey

¼ cup packed fresh basil leaves, sliced in a chiffonade (see Note, page 88)

6   Dust the prepared plank with cornmeal. Fold the pizza dough into thirds and carry it to the grill. Unroll the dough onto the prepared plank, folding up the edges so that the dough is the same size as the plank. Prick the dough all over with a fork, close the lid, and grill for 5 to 7 minutes, until the crust is lightly browned and crisp.

7   Open the grill lid and spread the bacon jam evenly over the crust. Top with the pepperoni slices and dollops of the ricotta mixture. Close the lid and grill until the cheese is golden and bubbly, 5 to 7 minutes. Transfer the pizza to a clean work surface and let cool for 10 minutes. Drizzle with the Hot Honey, sprinkle with the basil, slice, and serve.

MAKE IT AHEAD

The bacon jam can be made in advance and refrigerated in an airtight container for up to 2 weeks.

Fig, Prosciutto, and Gorgonzola Pizza

The combination of sweet figs, salty prosciutto, and umami Gorgonzola in every bite is perfection. **Serves 4**

1   At least 1 hour before grilling, soak your plank as directed on page 7.

2   Drain the figs and thinly slice them. Place them in a small bowl and toss them with the vinegar. Set aside.

3   Mix together the oil, garlic, fennel seeds, rosemary, salt, and pepper in another small bowl. Set aside.

4   Flour your work surface well. Stretch the dough with your hands as thinly as possible into a rectangle slightly larger than the plank. As you stretch the dough, move it around to prevent sticking. If the dough is springing back, let it rest for a few minutes, then resume stretching.

5   Preheat the grill and then the plank, and gather your equipment, as directed on page 15.

6   Dust the prepared plank with cornmeal. Fold the pizza dough into thirds and carry it to the grill. Unroll the dough onto the prepared plank, folding up the edges so that the dough is the same size as the plank. Prick the dough all over with a fork, close the lid, and grill for 5 to 7 minutes, until the crust is lightly browned and crisp.

7   Open the grill lid and brush the garlic-oil mixture evenly over the crust. Sprinkle with the mozzarella, then top with the prosciutto, figs, and Gorgonzola. Close the lid and grill until the cheese is golden and bubbly, 5 to 7 minutes. Transfer the pizza to a clean work surface and let cool for 10 minutes. Drizzle with the hot honey, slice, and serve.

12 dried Mission figs, soaked in a bowl of boiling hot water for 20 minutes

1 tablespoon balsamic vinegar

2 tablespoons extra virgin olive oil

1 garlic clove, minced

1 teaspoon fennel seeds

½ teaspoon chopped fresh rosemary

½ teaspoon kosher salt (see box, page 25)

¼ teaspoon freshly ground black pepper

All-purpose flour

8 to 9 ounces pizza dough, preferably New York–Style Dough (page 24), at room temperature

Coarse cornmeal

2 cups shredded low-moisture mozzarella

4 thin prosciutto slices

½ cup crumbled Gorgonzola

2 tablespoons Hot Honey (page 34) or store-bought hot honey

MAKE IT YOUR OWN

Try substituting Brie for the Gorgonzola.
You can also substitute dried apricots
or dried plums for dried figs. If you
prefer fresh fruit, try this with
fresh figs, fresh pears, or
fresh nectarines. (No need
to soak fresh fruit, so
you can skip that
step.)

Eggplant Caponata Pizza

Caponata is a Sicilian side dish consisting of slow-cooked vegetables—eggplant and tomato are the stars here—that lends itself as a delicious topping for a pizza. Drizzling the pizza with Balsamic Glaze (page 35) is the perfect final touch. **Serves 4**

1   At least 1 hour before grilling, soak your plank as directed on page 7.

2   Preheat the oven to 425°F.

3   To make the caponata, place the eggplant in a colander and season with 1 teaspoon of salt. Let it sit for 30 minutes.

4   Spread out the eggplant cubes on a baking sheet. Evenly drizzle 1 tablespoon of oil over the eggplant, sprinkle with ¼ teaspoon of black pepper, and toss. Roast for 30 to 35 minutes, stirring halfway through the cooking time, until deeply golden.

5   In the meantime, heat the remaining 1 tablespoon of oil in a medium saucepan over medium heat. Add the onion and bell pepper. Season with the remaining ¼ teaspoon of salt and ¼ teaspoon of black pepper. Cook, stirring often, until the vegetables are tender, 2 to 3 minutes.

6   Add the garlic and stir until fragrant, about 30 seconds. Add the tomato, olives, raisins, vinegar, capers, honey, and red pepper flakes. Stir to combine. Simmer, stirring occasionally, on medium-low heat until the mixture thickens slightly, 5 to 7 minutes.

7   Stir in the roasted eggplant and cook for another 2 to 3 minutes. Stir in half of the basil, then remove the pan from the heat and set aside.

For the Caponata

1 small Italian eggplant cut into 1-inch cubes

1¼ teaspoons kosher salt (see box, page 25)

2 tablespoons extra virgin olive oil

½ teaspoon freshly ground black pepper

½ cup chopped red onion

½ cup chopped red bell pepper

2 garlic cloves, minced

1 plum tomato, chopped

2 tablespoons chopped green olives, preferably Castelvetrano

2 tablespoons raisins

1½ tablespoons red wine vinegar

1 tablespoon capers, drained

1 tablespoon honey

¼ teaspoon red pepper flakes

½ cup packed fresh basil leaves, sliced in a chiffonade (see Note, page 88)

(ingredients continue)

8 To make the pizza, flour your work surface well. Stretch the dough with your hands as thinly as possible into a rectangle slightly larger than the plank. As you stretch the dough, move it around to prevent sticking. If the dough is springing back, let it rest for a few minutes, then resume stretching.

9 Preheat the grill and then the plank, and gather your equipment, as directed on page 15.

10 Dust the prepared plank with cornmeal. Fold the pizza dough into thirds and carry it to the grill. Unroll the dough onto the prepared plank, folding up the edges so that the dough is the same size as the plank. Prick the dough all over with a fork, close the lid, and grill for 5 to 7 minutes, until the crust is lightly browned and crisp.

11 Open the grill lid and sprinkle half of the mozzarella evenly over the crust. Top with the caponata mixture, remaining mozzarella, and pine nuts. Close the lid and grill until the cheese is golden and bubbly, 5 to 7 minutes. Transfer the pizza to a clean work surface and let cool for 10 minutes. Drizzle with the Balsamic Glaze, sprinkle with the remaining basil, slice, and serve.

For the Pizza

All-purpose flour

8 to 9 ounces pizza dough, preferably New York–Style Dough (page 24), at room temperature

Coarse cornmeal

2 cups shredded low-moisture mozzarella

1 tablespoon pine nuts, toasted (see box, page 33)

2 tablespoons Balsamic Glaze (page 35)

MAKE IT YOUR OWN
Swap out the pine nuts for toasted almonds or walnuts.

Al Pastor Pizza

Chile-marinated pork, sweet grilled pineapple, and oozing cheese—a must-try combination. The traditional annatto seed in the marinade is optional, but it imparts a beautiful red color to the meat and adds tang and aroma. Feel free to substitute an ancho chile for the guajillo (or vice versa), or use chili powder to taste, if necessary. **Serves 4**

1   To make the pork, place the guajillo and ancho chiles in a dry large skillet over medium-high heat and toast, turning until soft and pliable, about 2 minutes. Remove the skillet from the heat and stir in the reserved pineapple juice (it will boil immediately), and let it sit for 15 minutes.

2   Scrape the chiles and juice into a blender, along with the vinegar, garlic, oregano, paprika, annatto (if desired), salt, cumin, pepper, and cloves. Blend on high speed until combined and smooth. Pour the marinade into a resealable bag, add the pork, close the bag, and massage until the pork is covered with marinade on all sides. Refrigerate for 4 hours or up to overnight.

3   At least 1 hour before grilling, soak your plank as directed on page 7.

4   When ready to cook, heat the grill to medium-high heat, 475° to 500°F. Brush the grates with oil and remove the pork from the marinade. Grill the pork and the pineapple rings, flipping once, until grill marks appear, about 7 minutes for the pork and 1 to 2 minutes for the pineapple. Chop the pork and pineapple into ½-inch pieces. Set aside.

(continues)

For the Pork

1 guajillo chile, seeded (see box, page 44)

1 ancho chile, seeded

6 pineapple rings from a 20-oz can of sliced pineapple in juice, juice reserved (about 1 cup)

¼ cup white vinegar

3 garlic cloves

1 teaspoon dried oregano

1 teaspoon paprika

1 teaspoon ground annatto seeds (optional)

1 teaspoon kosher salt (see box, page 25)

½ teaspoon ground cumin

½ teaspoon freshly ground black pepper

¼ teaspoon ground cloves

1 pound boneless pork loin, cut crosswise into 4 slices

Canola oil

(ingredients continue)

5 To make the pizza, flour your work surface well. Stretch the dough with your hands as thinly as possible into a rectangle slightly larger than the plank. As you stretch the dough, move it around to prevent sticking. If the dough is springing back, let it rest for a few minutes, then resume stretching.

6 Preheat the plank, and gather your equipment, as directed on page 15.

7 Dust the prepared plank with cornmeal. Fold the pizza dough into thirds and carry it to the grill. Unroll the dough onto the prepared plank, folding up the edges so that the dough is the same size as the plank. Prick the dough all over with a fork, close the lid, and grill for 5 to 7 minutes, until the crust is lightly browned and crisp.

8 Open the grill lid and spread the salsa evenly over the crust. Sprinkle with the Monterey Jack, then top with the pork and pineapple. Close the lid and grill until the cheese is golden and bubbly, 5 to 7 minutes. Transfer the pizza to a clean work surface and let cool for 10 minutes. Sprinkle with the cilantro and green onion, drizzle with the lime juice, slice, and serve.

For the Pizza

All-purpose flour

8 to 9 ounces pizza dough, preferably Beer Pizza Dough (page 26), at room temperature

Coarse cornmeal

½ cup jarred salsa verde

2 cups shredded Monterey Jack

¼ cup chopped fresh cilantro

2 tablespoons sliced green onion, white and green parts

Juice of 1 lime

MAKE IT YOUR OWN

You can replace the pork with 1 pound of boneless, skinless chicken thighs, grilling them for about 10 minutes (longer for large pieces).

MAKE IT AHEAD

Make the marinade 2 days in advance and marinate the pork overnight.

Bacon, Cheddar, and Apple Pizza

Bacon and apples paired with the caramelized onions, grainy mustard, and creamy cheese make this pizza off-the-hook good when grilled on a plank. **Serves 4**

1 At least 1 hour before grilling, soak your plank as directed on page 7.

2 Cook the bacon in a 12-inch cast-iron skillet over medium heat, stirring occasionally, until the fat has rendered and the bacon is golden brown and crispy, 5 to 7 minutes. Transfer the bacon to a paper-towel-lined plate. Drain all but 1 tablespoon of bacon fat from the skillet. Add the onion, reduce the heat to medium, and cook, stirring occasionally, until the onion is golden brown, 4 to 5 minutes. Set aside.

3 Mix the mozzarella, Cheddar, and mustard in a medium bowl and set aside. Toss the apple pieces with the lemon juice and rosemary in a small bowl. Set aside.

4 Flour your work surface well. Stretch the dough with your hands as thinly as possible into a rectangle slightly larger than the plank. As you stretch the dough, move it around to prevent sticking. If the dough is springing back, let it rest for a few minutes, then resume stretching.

5 Preheat the grill and then the plank, and gather your equipment, as directed on page 15.

(continues)

8 ounces thick-cut bacon, cut into ¾-inch pieces

1 small onion, thinly sliced

1 cup shredded low-moisture mozzarella

1 cup shredded sharp Cheddar

2 tablespoons grainy Dijon mustard

1 small Fuji apple, cut into ½-inch pieces

1 teaspoon fresh lemon juice

1 teaspoon chopped fresh rosemary

All-purpose flour

8 to 9 ounces pizza dough, preferably New York–Style Dough (page 24), at room temperature

Coarse cornmeal

6 Dust the prepared plank with cornmeal. Fold the pizza dough into thirds and carry it to the grill. Unroll the dough onto the prepared plank, folding up the edges so that the dough is the same size as the plank. Prick the dough all over with a fork, close the lid, and grill for 5 to 7 minutes, until the crust is lightly browned and crisp.

7 Open the grill lid and spread the cheese mixture evenly over the crust. Top with the caramelized onion, bacon, and apple mixture. Close the lid and grill until the cheese is golden and bubbly, 5 to 7 minutes. Transfer the pizza to a clean work surface and let cool for 10 minutes. Slice and serve.

MAKE IT AHEAD

Cook the bacon and caramelized onion the day before. Bring them to room temperature before grilling the pizza.

Bacon, Goat Cheese, and Cherry Pizza

Topped with bourbon-infused cherries and crispy, thick-cut pieces of bacon, this pizza is a salty, sweet, smoky flavor bomb. **Serves 4**

1   At least 1 hour before grilling, soak your plank as directed on page 7.

2   Combine the dried cherries and bourbon in a small saucepan and bring to a boil over medium-high heat. Reduce the heat to low and simmer for 5 minutes. Set aside.

3   Cook the bacon in a 12-inch cast-iron skillet over medium heat, stirring occasionally, until the fat has rendered and the bacon is golden brown and crispy, 5 to 7 minutes. Transfer to a paper-towel-lined plate.

4   Flour your work surface well. Stretch the dough with your hands as thinly as possible into a rectangle slightly larger than the plank. As you stretch the dough, move it around to prevent sticking. If the dough is springing back, let it rest for a few minutes, then resume stretching.

5   Preheat the grill and then the plank, and gather your equipment, as directed on page 15.

6   Dust the prepared plank with cornmeal. Fold the pizza dough into thirds and carry it to the grill. Unroll the dough onto the prepared plank, folding up the edges so that the dough is the same size as the plank. Prick the dough all over with a fork, close the lid, and grill for 5 to 7 minutes, until the crust is lightly browned and crisp.

⅓ cup dried cherries

¼ cup bourbon

8 ounces thick-cut bacon, cut into 1-inch pieces

All-purpose flour

8 to 9 ounces pizza dough, preferably New York–Style Dough (page 24), at room temperature

Coarse cornmeal

1 cup shredded low-moisture mozzarella

1 cup crumbled goat cheese

2 tablespoons sliced green onion, white and green parts

7 Open the grill lid and sprinkle the mozzarella evenly over the crust. Top with the goat cheese, bacon, and bourbon-infused cherries. Close the lid and grill until the cheese is golden and bubbly, 5 to 7 minutes. Transfer the pizza to a clean work surface, sprinkle with the green onion, and let cool for 10 minutes. Slice and serve.

MAKE IT YOUR OWN

Substitute apple or orange juice for the bourbon. Or try feta instead of goat cheese if you have it on hand.

Steak and Blue Cheese Pizza

WITH BOURBON BALSAMIC GLAZE

Steak and blue cheese are a classic combination. Putting them on a planked pizza with caramelized onion, peppery arugula, and a sweet bourbon balsamic glaze takes that combination to another level. **Serves 4**

1 Combine the honey, vinegar, bourbon, mustard, sriracha, garlic, ½ teaspoon of salt, and ¼ teaspoon of pepper in a resealable plastic bag. Seal and shake to combine the ingredients. Add the steak to the bag, seal, and massage the steak until the marinade covers all sides. Refrigerate for 4 hours or up to overnight.

2 At least 1 hour before grilling, soak your plank as directed on page 7.

3 Toward the end of the soaking and marinating time, heat 1 tablespoon of the oil in a large skillet over medium-high heat. Add the onion, sugar, remaining ½ teaspoon of salt, and remaining ¼ teaspoon of pepper, stirring to coat. Cook, stirring occasionally, until the onion begins to soften, about 5 minutes. Reduce the heat to medium-low and cook, stirring frequently, until the onion is caramelized and jammy, 15 to 20 minutes.

4 Remove the steak from the marinade, shaking off any excess, and set aside. Pour the marinade into a small saucepan, bring to a boil, then reduce the heat to medium-low and simmer until it becomes a thick, syrupy glaze, 5 to 10 minutes. Remove it from the heat and set aside.

⅓ cup honey

⅓ cup balsamic vinegar

2 tablespoons bourbon or other whiskey

1 tablespoon Dijon mustard

1 teaspoon sriracha

2 garlic cloves, minced

1 teaspoon kosher salt (see box, page 25)

½ teaspoon freshly ground black pepper

8 ounces skirt or flank steak

1 tablespoon extra virgin olive oil, plus more for greasing the grill grates

1 small onion, halved and thinly sliced

1 teaspoon sugar

All-purpose flour

8 to 9 ounces pizza dough, preferably New York–Style Dough (page 24), at room temperature

Coarse cornmeal

2 cups shredded low-moisture mozzarella

½ cup crumbled blue cheese

1 cup loosely packed arugula

5 When ready to cook, heat the grill to medium-high heat, about 475° to 500°F. Brush the grates with oil and grill the steak until the edges are crisp, 2 to 4 minutes. Flip the steak and grill another 3 to 4 minutes, until nicely crusted. Let the steak rest for 10 minutes, then cut into ½-inch strips and set aside. If using flank steak, remember to slice across the grain.

6 Flour your work surface well. Stretch the dough with your hands as thinly as possible into a rectangle slightly larger than the plank. As you stretch the dough, move it around to prevent sticking. If the dough is springing back, let it rest for a few minutes, then resume stretching.

7 Preheat the grill and then the plank, and gather your equipment, as directed on page 15.

8 Dust the prepared plank with cornmeal. Fold the pizza dough into thirds and carry it to the grill. Unroll the dough onto the prepared plank, folding up the edges so that the dough is the same size as the plank. Prick the dough all over with a fork, close the lid, and grill for 5 to 7 minutes, until the crust is lightly browned and crisp.

9 Open the grill lid and spread the mozzarella and blue cheese evenly over the crust. Top with the caramelized onion and steak. Close the lid and grill until the cheese is golden and bubbly, 5 to 7 minutes. Transfer the pizza to a clean work surface and let cool for 10 minutes. Top with the arugula, drizzle with the bourbon balsamic glaze, slice, and serve.

MAKE IT AHEAD

The caramelized onion can be made and the steak can be marinated the day before. Just bring both to room temperature before grilling.

Salmon and Kale Pizza

WITH CRISPY COCONUT AND RUM GLAZE

The smoke flavor imparted by the grilling plank pairs very well with salmon. Topped with coconut and the most delicious rum glaze, this pizza may not be traditional, but it is outrageously delicious. **Serves 4**

1 At least 1 hour before grilling, soak your plank as directed on page 7.

2 Prepare the glaze by melting the butter in a small saucepan over medium heat. Stir in ¼ cup of rum, the molasses, and 3 tablespoons of brown sugar and bring to a boil. Reduce the heat to medium-low and simmer until syrupy, about 3 minutes. Set aside.

3 Heat the coconut oil in a large skillet over medium-high heat. Add the onion, the remaining 2 teaspoons of brown sugar, 1 teaspoon of salt, and ½ teaspoon of pepper, stirring to coat. Cook, stirring occasionally, until the onion begins to soften, about 3 minutes. Reduce the heat to medium-low and cook, stirring frequently, until the onion is caramelized and jammy, 15 to 20 minutes. Add the remaining ¼ cup of rum and cook for 1 to 2 minutes, until most of the liquid has cooked off. Remove from the heat and set aside.

4 Mix the kale and mozzarella in a large bowl until combined and set aside.

5 Gently toss the salmon strips with 2 tablespoons of rum glaze, the remaining ½ teaspoon of salt, and ¼ teaspoon of pepper in a medium bowl and set aside.

6 Combine the jalapeño and coconut flakes in a small bowl and set aside.

(continues)

2 tablespoons unsalted butter

½ cup rum

2 tablespoons molasses

3 tablespoons plus 2 teaspoons light brown sugar

2 tablespoons coconut oil

1 small red onion, halved and thinly sliced

1½ teaspoons kosher salt (see box, page 25)

¾ teaspoon freshly ground black pepper

1 cup shredded kale

2 cups shredded low-moisture mozzarella

1 pound salmon, thinly sliced against the grain into strips ¼ inch thick

1 jalapeño, seeded and finely diced (see box, page 44)

⅓ cup unsweetened coconut flakes

All-purpose flour

8 to 9 ounces pizza dough, preferably New York–Style Dough (page 24), at room temperature

Coarse cornmeal

7 Flour your work surface well. Stretch the dough with your hands as thinly as possible into a rectangle slightly larger than the plank. As you stretch the dough, move it around to prevent sticking. If the dough is springing back, let it rest for a few minutes, then resume stretching.

8 Preheat the grill and then the plank, and gather your equipment, as directed on page 15.

9 Dust the prepared plank with cornmeal. Fold the pizza dough into thirds and carry it to the grill. Unroll the dough onto the prepared plank, folding up the edges so that the dough is the same size as the plank. Prick the dough all over with a fork, close the lid, and grill for 5 to 7 minutes, until the crust is lightly browned and crisp.

10 Open the grill lid and spread the caramelized onion evenly over the crust. Sprinkle with the cheese and kale mixture, then top with the salmon slices and sprinkle with the coconut mixture. Close the lid and grill until the cheese is golden and bubbly and the fish is cooked, 5 to 7 minutes. Transfer the pizza to a clean work surface and let cool for 10 minutes. Drizzle with the remaining rum glaze and let cool for 10 minutes. Slice and serve.

MAKE IT YOUR OWN

Swap out the kale for other leafy greens, such as spinach or chard.

MAKE IT AHEAD

The rum glaze and caramelized onion can be prepared a day in advance. Bring them to room temperature before grilling the pizza. Warm the glaze reserved for drizzling on the pizza in the microwave for 15 seconds before using.

Roasted Cauliflower and Ricotta Pizza
WITH OLIVES, RAISINS, AND CAPERS

This pizza has such wonderful contrasting flavors: Briny olives and capers, sweet raisins, and caramelized cauliflower atop creamy ricotta and mozzarella, all infused with woodsmoke. Wear your eating pants! **Serves 4**

1 At least 1 hour before grilling, soak your plank as directed on page 7.

2 Preheat the oven to 425°F.

3 To make the cauliflower, place the florets on a baking sheet and toss with the oil, salt, and pepper. Roast for 25 to 30 minutes, tossing the florets a few times, until they are tender and browned. Set aside to cool for 10 minutes.

4 Transfer the florets to a large bowl and stir in the capers, olives, raisins, vinegar, and honey.

5 To make the pizza, combine the ricotta, mozzarella, Parmesan, lemon zest and juice, garlic, oregano, salt, and pepper in a medium bowl and mix well.

6 Flour your work surface well. Stretch the dough with your hands as thinly as possible into a rectangle slightly larger than the plank. As you stretch the dough, move it around to prevent sticking. If the dough is springing back, let it rest for a few minutes, then resume stretching.

7 Preheat the grill and then the plank, and gather your equipment, as directed on page 15.

(continues)

For the Cauliflower

½ small head of cauliflower, cut into florets (see Note, page 128)

2 tablespoons extra virgin olive oil

1 teaspoon kosher salt (see box, page 25)

¼ teaspoon freshly ground black pepper

¼ cup capers

¼ cup pitted and chopped green olives

¼ cup raisins

1 tablespoon sherry vinegar

1 tablespoon honey

For the Pizza

1 cup ricotta

1 cup shredded low-moisture mozzarella

¼ cup freshly grated Parmesan

1 lemon, zested and juiced

2 garlic cloves, minced

¼ teaspoon dried oregano

¼ teaspoon kosher salt (see box, page 25)

(ingredients continue)

8 Dust the prepared plank with cornmeal. Fold the pizza dough into thirds and carry it to the grill. Unroll the dough onto the prepared plank, folding up the edges so that the dough is the same size as the plank. Prick the dough all over with a fork, close the lid, and grill for 5 to 7 minutes, until the crust is lightly browned and crisp.

9 Open the grill lid and spread the ricotta mixture evenly over the crust. Scatter the cauliflower mixture over the ricotta. Close the lid and grill until the cheese is golden and bubbly and the cauliflower is warmed through, 5 to 7 minutes. Transfer the pizza to a clean work surface and let cool for 10 minutes. Sprinkle with the parsley, slice, and serve.

Note: *Do yourself a favor and roast the remaining half cauliflower while making this recipe so you have some to munch on while preparing the rest of the ingredients.*

¼ teaspoon freshly ground black pepper

All-purpose flour

8 to 9 ounces pizza dough, preferably New York–Style Dough (page 24), at room temperature

Coarse cornmeal

2 tablespoons chopped fresh flat-leaf parsley

MAKE IT YOUR OWN

This pizza is also really good with some crumbled bacon sprinkled on top.

MAKE IT AHEAD

The cauliflower can be roasted and tossed with the capers, olives, raisins, vinegar, and honey the day before. The ricotta mixture can also be prepared the day before.

Aleppo Pepper, Lemon, and Cilantro Shrimp Pizza

Aleppo pepper, named after the Syrian city of Aleppo and made from the deep red Halaby chile, is fruity, tangy, a little bit spicy, and it pairs well with the smoke and wood of planked pizzas. **Serves 4**

1 At least 1 hour before grilling, soak your plank as directed on page 7.

2 Season the shrimp with the Aleppo pepper and salt. Heat 1 tablespoon of oil in a large skillet over medium-high heat. Add the shrimp and cook for 1 minute on each side. Transfer the shrimp to a cutting board and cut into ½-inch pieces. The shrimp will not be cooked through yet, so don't worry if it still looks somewhat gray and translucent.

3 Heat the remaining 2 tablespoons of oil in the skillet over medium heat. Add the garlic, cilantro, and lemon juice and sauté until the liquid evaporates, about 1 minute. Remove from the heat and toss in a medium bowl with the shrimp. Set aside.

4 Flour your work surface well. Stretch the dough with your hands as thinly as possible into a rectangle slightly larger than the plank. As you stretch the dough, move it around to prevent sticking. If the dough is springing back, let it rest for a few minutes, then resume stretching.

5 Preheat the grill and then the plank, and gather your equipment, as directed on page 15.

12 ounces large shrimp, peeled and deveined

2 teaspoons ground Aleppo pepper

1 teaspoon kosher salt (see box, page 25)

3 tablespoons extra virgin olive oil

4 garlic cloves, minced

1 bunch fresh cilantro, chopped

2 tablespoons fresh lemon juice

All-purpose flour

8 to 9 ounces pizza dough, preferably Neapolitan-Style Dough (page 22), at room temperature

Coarse cornmeal

2 cups shredded low-moisture mozzarella

6 Dust the prepared plank with cornmeal. Fold the pizza dough into thirds and carry it to the grill. Unroll the dough onto the prepared plank, folding up the edges so that the dough is the same size as the plank. Prick the dough all over with a fork, close the lid, and grill for 5 to 7 minutes, until the crust is lightly browned and crisp.

7 Open the grill lid and sprinkle the mozzarella evenly over the crust. Top with the shrimp mixture. Close the lid and grill until the cheese is golden and bubbly, 5 to 7 minutes. Transfer the pizza to a clean work surface and let cool for 10 minutes. Slice and serve.

MAKE IT YOUR OWN

You can swap out the shrimp with 6 to 8 ounces of chicken breast. And feel free to play around with other chile powders in place of the Aleppo, such as chipotle or ancho chile powder. You can also try other smooth, creamy cheeses on this pizza, like Fontina, Monterey Jack, provolone, or Gouda.

Sweet
Pizzas

When describing food, the words *sweet* and *smoky* typically evoke images of barbecue meats, sauces, and rubs. In this chapter, it's dessert pizza. Toss your dough onto the plank and start on your dessert pie directly after your last savory pie to keep the pizza party going. Dessert pizzas contain flavors presented in subtle, complex ways. Topped with fruit, chocolate, nuts, or my personal favorite, marshmallows, they'll take your dessert game to the next level.

I'm always looking for a twist on an old favorite, and turning candied yams into a smoky Sweet Potato and Marshmallow Pizza (page 141) is exactly the right twist. Most fruit, including strawberries, apples, pears, peaches, plums, apricots, and cherries, tastes amazing on a plank-grilled pizza. Berries don't usually need to be roasted in advance since they soften quickly on the grill, but roasting most other fruit reduces moisture that might make the dough soggy. Plus, the sweet caramelization that results from roasting pairs perfectly with the smokiness of the plank. And since the ingredients for planked pizzas can be prepared in advance, these sweet pizzas are also excellent party food. They come together quickly when it's time for dessert. Your guests will be thrilled with the results, and you'll be thrilled with the ease.

Nutella, Honey, and Blue Cheese Pizza

Nutella and blue cheese? On pizza? Trust me, on a plank-grilled crust, topped with walnuts and drizzled with honey, the pairing is unforgettably good. **Serves 4**

1 At least 1 hour before grilling, soak your plank as directed on page 7.

2 Flour your work surface well. Stretch the dough with your hands as thinly as possible into a rectangle slightly larger than the plank. As you stretch the dough, move it around to prevent sticking. If the dough is springing back, let it rest for a few minutes, then resume stretching.

3 Preheat the grill and then the plank, and gather your equipment, as directed on page 15.

4 Dust the prepared plank with cornmeal. Fold the pizza dough into thirds and carry it to the grill. Unroll the dough onto the prepared plank, folding up the edges so that the dough is the same size as the plank. Prick the dough all over with a fork, close the lid, and grill for 5 to 7 minutes, until the crust is lightly browned and crisp.

5 Open the grill lid and spread the chocolate hazelnut spread evenly over the crust. Sprinkle with the blue cheese and walnuts. Close the lid and grill until the cheese has melted and the nuts are toasted, about 5 minutes. Transfer the pizza to a clean work surface and let cool for 10 minutes. Drizzle with the honey, sprinkle with the sea salt, slice, and serve.

All-purpose flour

8 to 9 ounces pizza dough, preferably New York–Style Dough (page 24), at room temperature

Coarse cornmeal

¾ cup chocolate hazelnut spread, preferably Nutella

½ cup crumbled blue cheese

¼ cup chopped walnuts

2 tablespoons honey

¼ teaspoon flaky sea salt

MAKE IT YOUR OWN

Swap out the walnuts for chopped almonds.

Strawberry Pizza
WITH MINT AND LEMON GLAZE

Fruit is wonderful on plank-grilled pizzas because the technique brings out its natural sweetness. Combining sweet-tart strawberries with refreshing mint and a tangy lemon glaze, you can't go wrong. **Serves 4**

1 At least 1 hour before grilling, soak your plank as directed on page 7.

2 Whisk together the sugar, lemon juice, water, cornstarch, and salt in a small saucepan over medium heat. Bring the mixture to a boil, whisking constantly, then reduce the heat to low and cook for an additional 30 seconds, or until it thickens. Remove from the heat and stir in the zest and vanilla.

3 Set aside 3 tablespoons of glaze in a small bowl.

4 Stir together the remaining glaze and ricotta in a medium bowl.

5 Flour your work surface well. Stretch the dough with your hands as thinly as possible into a rectangle slightly larger than the plank. As you stretch the dough, move it around to prevent sticking. If the dough is springing back, let it rest for a few minutes, then resume stretching.

6 Preheat the grill and then the plank, and gather your equipment, as directed on page 15.

(continues)

¼ cup sugar

⅓ cup fresh lemon juice

¼ cup water

½ tablespoon cornstarch

Pinch of kosher salt (see box, page 25)

Zest of 1 lemon

½ teaspoon vanilla extract

1 cup ricotta

All-purpose flour

8 to 9 ounces pizza dough, preferably New York–Style Dough (page 24), at room temperature

Coarse cornmeal

1 cup shredded low-moisture mozzarella

1 pint medium strawberries, hulled and quartered

¼ cup fresh mint leaves, sliced in a chiffonade (see Note, page 88)

7 Dust the prepared plank with cornmeal. Fold the pizza dough into thirds and carry it to the grill. Unroll the dough onto the prepared plank, folding up the edges so that the dough is the same size as the plank. Prick the dough all over with a fork, close the lid, and grill for 5 to 7 minutes, until the crust is lightly browned and crisp.

8 Open the grill lid and spread the ricotta mixture evenly over the crust. Sprinkle with the mozzarella, then top with the strawberries. Close the lid and grill until the mozzarella is melted and bubbly, 5 to 7 minutes. Transfer the pizza to a clean work surface and drizzle with the reserved glaze. If the glaze has set up, microwave it for 10 seconds until pourable. Let the pizza cool for 10 minutes. Sprinkle with the mint, slice, and serve.

MAKE IT YOUR OWN
Swap out the mint for tarragon or basil.

S'mores Pizza

Traditional s'mores are no stranger to woodsmoke, so it's only natural that silky chocolate and gooey marshmallows taste great on a smoky, charred pizza crust. Make sure to check your pizza a couple of minutes after adding the toppings. The marshmallows, chocolate, and nuts (if using) can burn easily. **Serves 4**

1 At least 1 hour before grilling, soak your plank as directed on page 7.

2 Combine the graham cracker crumbs and butter in a medium bowl. Set aside.

3 Flour your work surface well. Stretch the dough with your hands as thinly as possible into a rectangle slightly larger than the plank. As you stretch the dough, move it around to prevent sticking. If the dough is springing back, let it rest for a few minutes, then resume stretching.

4 Preheat the grill and then the plank, and gather your equipment, as directed on page 15.

5 Dust the prepared plank with cornmeal. Fold the pizza dough into thirds and carry it to the grill. Unroll the dough onto the prepared plank, folding up the edges so that the dough is the same size as the plank. Prick the dough all over with a fork, close the lid, and grill for 5 to 7 minutes, until the crust is lightly browned and crisp.

6 Open the grill lid and sprinkle the chocolate chips, marshmallows, graham cracker mixture, and almonds, if desired, over the crust. Close the lid and grill for 2 to 3 minutes, until the chocolate has just melted and the marshmallows are golden. Transfer the pizza to a clean work surface and let cool for 5 minutes. Slice and serve.

8 graham cracker squares, ground to crumbs in a food processor

2 tablespoons unsalted butter, melted

All-purpose flour

8 to 9 ounces pizza dough, preferably New York–Style Dough (page 24), at room temperature

Coarse cornmeal

½ cup semisweet chocolate chips

1 cup miniature marshmallows

¼ cup sliced almonds (optional)

MAKE IT YOUR OWN
Swap out the sweet potato for canned pumpkin puree, and turn this pizza into an homage to pumpkin pie with a meringue crust.

Sweet Potato and Marshmallow Pizza

This pizza tastes like candied yams with marshmallows toasted over a campfire. So good! **Serves 4**

1 At least 1 hour before grilling, soak your plank as directed on page 7.

2 Place the sweet potato in a medium saucepan, and cover with water. Bring to a boil over high heat, then reduce the heat to medium and simmer until the sweet potato is tender, 8 to 10 minutes. Drain and return the pieces to the saucepan. Add the brown sugar, orange juice, salt, and cinnamon and mash with a potato masher until smooth. Set aside.

3 Flour your work surface well. Stretch the dough with your hands as thinly as possible into a rectangle slightly larger than the plank. As you stretch the dough, move it around to prevent sticking. If the dough is springing back, let it rest for a few minutes, then resume stretching.

4 Preheat the grill and then the plank, and gather your equipment, as directed on page 15.

5 Dust the prepared plank with cornmeal. Fold the pizza dough into thirds and carry it to the grill. Unroll the dough onto the prepared plank, folding up the edges so that the dough is the same size as the plank. Prick the dough all over with a fork, close the lid, and grill for 5 to 7 minutes, until the crust is lightly browned and crisp.

6 Open the grill lid and spread the sweet potato mixture evenly over the crust. Sprinkle with the pecans, then top with the marshmallows. Close the lid and grill until the marshmallows have puffed and turned brown, 2 to 3 minutes. Transfer the pizza to a clean work surface and let cool for 10 minutes. Slice and serve.

1 medium sweet potato or yam, peeled and cut into 1-inch chunks

2 tablespoons light brown sugar

1 tablespoon orange juice

⅛ teaspoon kosher salt, (see box, page 25)

⅛ teaspoon ground cinnamon

All-purpose flour

8 to 9 ounces pizza dough, preferably New York–Style Dough (page 24), at room temperature

Coarse cornmeal

¼ cup pecan halves, toasted then chopped (see box, page 33)

12 large marshmallows

MAKE IT AHEAD

The sweet potato mixture can be prepared a day in advance—just bring it to room temperature before grilling the pizzas.

Caramel Apple Pizza

This luscious, satisfying pizza combines apples, caramel, chocolate, and a crispy, chewy crust. Keep a close eye on the nuts so they don't burn. **Serves 4**

1 At least 1 hour before grilling, soak your plank as directed on page 7.

2 Mix together the apples and lemon juice in a large bowl. Melt the butter in a large stainless-steel skillet over medium-high heat. Stir in the apples, brown sugar, and cinnamon and sauté, stirring occasionally, until the apples are tender, 7 to 10 minutes.

3 Flour your work surface well. Stretch the dough with your hands as thinly as possible into a rectangle slightly larger than the plank. As you stretch the dough, move it around to prevent sticking. If the dough is springing back, let it rest for a few minutes, then resume stretching.

4 Preheat the grill and then the plank, and gather your equipment, as directed on page 15.

5 Dust the prepared plank with cornmeal. Fold the pizza dough into thirds and carry it to the grill. Unroll the dough onto the prepared plank, folding up the edges so that the dough is the same size as the plank. Prick the dough all over with a fork, close the lid, and grill for 5 to 7 minutes, until the crust is lightly browned and crisp.

6 Open the grill lid and use a slotted spoon to spread the apple mixture over the crust, leaving behind any juices in the pan so the crust does not become soggy. Sprinkle with the chocolate and almonds. Close the lid and grill until the chocolate has melted, taking care that the chocolate and nuts do not burn, 2 to 3 minutes. Transfer the pizza to a clean work surface and let cool for 10 minutes. Drizzle with the caramel sauce, slice, and serve.

2 Granny Smith apples peeled, cored, and sliced ¼ inch thick

1 tablespoon fresh lemon juice

2 tablespoons unsalted butter

¼ cup packed light brown sugar

½ teaspoon ground cinnamon

All-purpose flour

8 to 9 ounces pizza dough, preferably New York–Style Dough (page 24), at room temperature

Coarse cornmeal

¼ cup coarsely chopped semisweet chocolate

¼ cup sliced almonds

2 tablespoons caramel ice-cream topping

Conversion Tables

APPROXIMATE EQUIVALENTS

1 stick butter = 8 tbs = 4 oz = ½ cup = 115 g

1 cup all-purpose presifted flour = 4.5 oz

1 cup granulated sugar = 7 oz = about 200 g

1 cup (firmly packed) brown sugar = 7½ oz = 215 g

1 cup powdered sugar = 3¾ oz = 115 g

1 cup honey or syrup = 12 oz

1 cup grated cheese = 4 oz

1 cup dried beans = 8 oz

1 large egg = about 2 oz or about 3 tbs

1 egg yolk = about 1 tbs

1 egg white = about 2 tbs

Please note that all conversions are approximate but close enough to be useful when converting from one system to another.

WEIGHT CONVERSIONS

US/UK	METRIC	US/UK	METRIC
½ oz	15 g	7 oz	200 g
1 oz	30 g	8 oz	230 g
1½ oz	45 g	9 oz	250 g
2 oz	60 g	10 oz	280 g
2½ oz	75 g	11 oz	310 g
3 oz	90 g	12 oz	340 g
3½ oz	100 g	13 oz	370 g
4 oz	115 g	14 oz	400 g
5 oz	140 g	15 oz	425 g
6 oz	170 g	1 lb	450 g

LIQUID CONVERSIONS

US	IMPERIAL	METRIC
2 tbs	1 fl oz	30 ml
3 tbs	1½ fl oz	45 ml
¼ cup	2 fl oz	60 ml
⅓ cup	2½ fl oz	75 ml
⅓ cup + 1 tbs	3 fl oz	90 ml
⅓ cup + 2 tbs	3½ fl oz	100 ml
½ cup	4 fl oz	125 ml
⅔ cup	5 fl oz	150 ml
¾ cup	6 fl oz	175 ml
¾ cup + 2 tbs	7 fl oz	200 ml
1 cup	8 fl oz	250 ml
1 cup + 2 tbs	9 fl oz	275 ml
1¼ cups	10 fl oz	300 ml
1⅓ cups	11 fl oz	325 ml
1½ cups	12 fl oz	350 ml
1⅔ cups	13 fl oz	375 ml
1¾ cups	14 fl oz	400 ml
1¾ cups + 2 tbs	15 fl oz	450 ml
2 cups (1 pint)	16 fl oz	475 ml
2½ cups	20 fl oz (1 pint)	600 ml
3¾ cups	1½ pints	900 ml
4 cups	1¾ pints	1 liter

OVEN TEMPERATURES

°F	GAS MARK	°C	°F	GAS MARK	°C
250	½	120	400	6	200
275	1	140	425	7	220
300	2	150	450	8	230
325	3	160	475	9	240
350	4	180	500	10	260
375	5	190			

Note: *Reduce the temperature by 68°F (20°C) for fan-assisted ovens.*

Index

Thank You!

First and foremost, I want to thank my brother, Sam Nassar, for starting me on this plank grilling journey nearly twenty years and four cookbooks ago. I love you.

To my good friend Laura Howell, who tried nearly every recipe in this book, even some over and over until they were right, thank you for bringing this vision to life. Your feedback, suggestions, support, and love mean more than words to me.

A huge thank-you to all my recipe testers: Kim, Nikkie, and Zoe Ball; Mike and Michelle Derr; Kelly and Greg Cederstrom; Mike and Michele Piazzoni; Tom and Sue Jas; Mike, Leslie, and Sean Woods; Kevin LaCasse; Anders ("all this pizza needs is a little acid") Swanson; and Cindy LaCasse. You all have left your mark on these pizzas, and I'm so grateful for all your feedback and support.

To my son, Andrew, who would call me from across the country while I was writing this cookbook to check in on me and talk me through recipes with suggestions and great advice, thank you from the bottom of my heart. Your passion and talent for cooking make me so proud.

Most important, a big thank-you to my husband, Roland. The number of dishes you washed during the making of this book would fill an Olympic-size pool, and you did it with a smile on your face the whole time. You said it was because you got to eat pizza nearly every day, but your support and belief in me has always been unwavering and unconditional. I'm grateful and so blessed you're my life partner. I love you.

About the Author

Dina Guillen is the author of *Plank Grilling* and coauthor of *The Plank Grilling Cookbook* and *Cooking Club*. In addition to her three cookbooks, she has created recipes for *Cooking Light* magazine. When she's not writing cookbooks, she is the Director of Marketing for a Northern California taco restaurant chain called Jimboy's Tacos, as well as wife to her husband, Roland, and mother to her son, Andrew.